Surf's Up!

Read the passage and follow the directions below.

Surfers are always looking for the best waves. This search for the perfect wave is called a surf **safari.** For many surfers, a surf safari takes them to the beaches of Hawaii. In fact, the sport of surfing began in Hawaii. The person who made surfing popular around the world was a Hawaiian man named Duke Kahanamoku.

People say that Duke Kahanamoku is the father of modern surfing. He grew up in Hawaii, swimming and surfing almost every day. He was so good at swimming, he won five Olympic medals for it! Some people called him The Human Fish. Duke loved swimming, but he loved surfing even more.

Duke shared the sport of surfing with others. He also showed people that surfboards can save lives. One day, he was having a picnic on the beach in Newport Beach, California. He saw a boat **capsize** at sea, and people fell into the water. Duke made three trips to the boat on his surfboard. He took eight people back to shore and saved their lives!

People remember Duke as a great athlete and a kind person. In fact, there is even a postal stamp with a picture of Duke Kahanamoku on it!

Use context clues to figure out the meaning of each word.
Circle the correct meaning.

1. safari
    a) a long surfboard
    b) a search or hunt
    c) a perfect beach
2. capsize
    a) to save someone's life
    b) to surf on big waves
    c) to flip over in the water

Read each statement and write **true** or **false**.

3. The sport of surfing began in Newport Beach. _____
4. Surfers go on a surf safari to find the best waves. _____
5. Duke Kahanamoku won three gold medals for surfing. _____
6. Duke Kahanamoku used his surfboard to rescue people. _____

Times by 2

Look at the symbol in each problem. Check the code to find the corresponding number. Then write out and solve the problem.

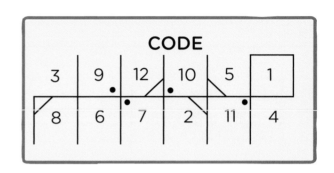

1. 2 x ⌟

   2 x ___ = ___

2. 2 x ⌐

   2 x ___ = ___

3. 2 x ⌊•⌋

   2 x ___ = ___

4. 2 x ⟍⌐

   2 x ___ = ___

5. 2 x ⌊⟋

   2 x ___ = ___

6. 2 x ⌐⌐

   2 x ___ = ___

7. 2 x ⌈•⌉

   2 x ___ = ___

8. 2 x □

   2 x ___ = ___

9. 2 x ⌐•

   2 x ___ = ___

10. 2 x ⌐⟍

    2 x ___ = ___

11. 2 x ⟍⌊

    2 x ___ = ___

12. 2 x ⌊•⌋

    2 x ___ = ___

SUMMER STUDY

GRADE 4

FlashKids

New York

New York

An Imprint of Sterling Publishing
1166 Avenue of the Americas
New York, NY 10036

ISBN 978-1-4114-7860-2

Distributed in Canada by Sterling Publishing Co., Inc.
c/o Canadian Manda Group, 664 Annette Street
Toronto, Ontario, Canada M6S 2C8
Distributed in the United Kingdom by GMC Distribution Services
Castle Place, 166 High Street, Lewes, East Sussex, England BN7 1XU
Distributed in Australia by Capricorn Link (Australia) Pty. Ltd.
P.O. Box 704, Windsor, NSW 2756, Australia

For information about custom editions, special sales, and premium
and corporate purchases, please contact Sterling Special Sales at
800-805-5489 or specialsales@sterlingpublishing.com.

Manufactured in Canada
Lot #:
2 4 6 8 10 9 7 5 3 1
03/16

www.flashkids.com

Dear Parent,

As a parent, you want your child to have time to relax and have fun during the summer, but you don't want your child's math and reading skills to get rusty. How do you make time for summer fun and also ensure that your child will be ready for the next school year?

This Summer Study workbook provides short, fun activities to help children keep their skills fresh all summer long. This book not only reviews what children learned during third grade, it also introduces what they'll be learning in fourth grade. Best of all, the games, puzzles, and stories help children retain their knowledge as well as build new skills. By the time your child finishes the book, he or she will be ready for a smooth transition into fourth grade.

As your child completes the activities in this book, shower him or her with encouragement and praise. You can feel good knowing that you are taking an active and important role in your child's education. Helping your child complete the activities in this book is providing an excellent example—that you value learning every day! Have a wonderful summer, and most of all, have fun learning together!

A Story of Nouns

A **noun** names a person, a place, or a thing. Read the story. Circle all the nouns. Then list them below as a person, a place, or a thing. Hint: Some nouns are used more than once. Circle them, but list them only once.

Have you ever seen a wild bear? You might have been camping or taking a hike. It can be exciting, but also a little scary. Last summer in Coal Canyon, Josh Baker was hiking with his friend Carlos Gomez. They stopped to eat lunch in a meadow. While they were eating, Carlos saw something moving in the brush. He thought it might be a bear. He told Josh to get up and leave the food.

"Back away slowly," he said. "Whatever you do, don't run."

The boys got to their feet as the bear came closer.

"Can he smell our food?" Josh asked.

"Bears can smell really well," Carlos replied. "It probably smelled our food."

Josh and Carlos backed away very slowly, facing the bear. As soon as they got back to camp, they reported the bear to a forest ranger. This helped keep both the campers and the bear safe. These boys did the right thing. Always remember, if you respect a bear, it will respect you.

PERSON	PLACE	THING
_____ _____	_____	_____ _____
_____ _____	_____	_____ _____
_____ _____	_____	_____ _____
		_____ _____

Finding Opposites

Read each sentence. Find the word in the box that means the opposite of the underlined word. Write it on the line.

horrible	calm
awake	winter
over	slowly
noisy	careful
sour	spend

1. The lemonade was almost too <u>sweet</u>.   _____

2. The kittens are <u>asleep</u> in the basket.   _____

3. Shana can be <u>careless</u> with her things.   _____

4. Brett found his hat <u>under</u> the bed.   _____

5. We try to <u>save</u> a little money each week.   _____

6. I love warm <u>summer</u> nights full of stars.   _____

7. <u>Wild</u> winds blew through the trees.   _____

8. My dad is a <u>wonderful</u> cook.   _____

9. The <u>quiet</u> baby played in her crib.   _____

10. The boy walked <u>quickly</u> along the beach.   _____

Round Off Roundup!

Round each number to the nearest ten, hundred, or thousand.

Tens

1. 38   _40_

2. 56   _____

3. 422   _____

4. 6,549   _____

5. 853   _____

Hundreds

6. 345   _300_

7. 678   _____

8. 8,211   _____

9. 1,395   _____

10. 84   _____

Thousands

11. 4,165   _4,000_

12. 3,902   _____

13. 2,844   _____

14. 7,249   _____

15. 931   _____

Target Practice

Fill in each target using numbers **0–12**. Write each number only once so that the sum of each row hits the target number in the center.
Hint: Not all numbers will be used in all targets.

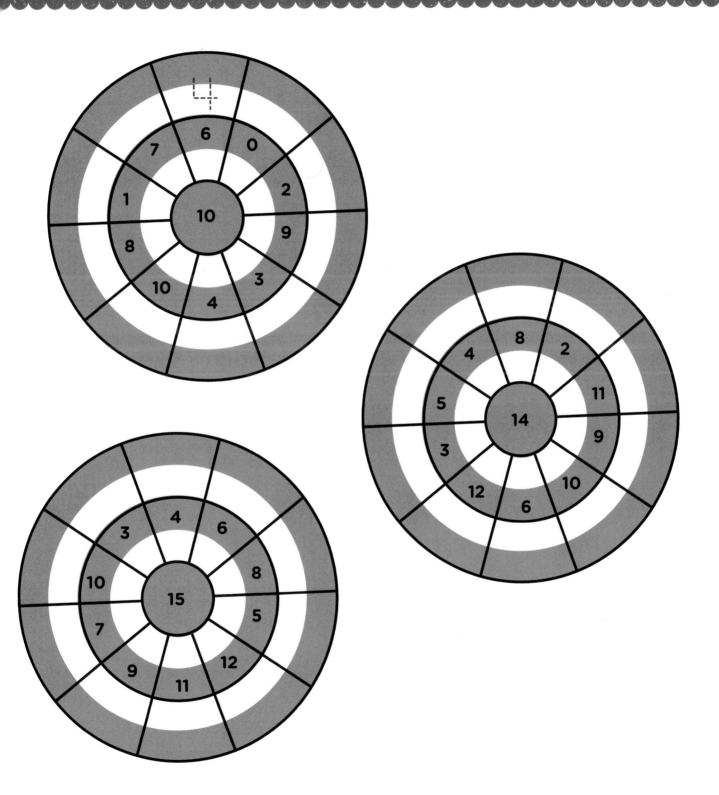

Which Word?

Read the words in ( ). They sound the same but have different meanings and spellings. Write the correct words to complete each sentence.

1. Kit's _____ wags whenever I call to him. (tale, tail)

2. The _____ of fresh baked bread filled the house. (sent, scent)

3. My _____ took us to the zoo last Saturday. (aunt, ant)

4. May I have a _____ of apple pie? (piece, peace)

5. Jun _____ her own dress for the school dance. (maid, made)

6. Manny and Lisa _____ horses on the ranch. (rode, road)

7. What kinds of _____ should we bring to camp? (close, clothes)

8. The big _____ whale swam right next to our boat. (blue, blew)

9. Make sure not to _____ that costly vase. (brake, break)

10. I watered _____ plants while they were gone. (their, there)

Happy Birthday Homonyms

Fill in the sentence with the correct word from the word box.

Dear	through	blue	ate	scent	creak
deer	threw	blew	eight	sent	creek

Dear _____ Grandma,

I got the card you _____ me for my birthday. Yesterday I turned _____ years old. We went on a hike _____ the woods. It was a beautiful day, and the _____ of wildflowers was in the air. We even saw a _____ ! We came to a _____ with clear, _____ water. As we walked across the bridge, I heard it _____ . At lunchtime, we stopped for a picnic and _____ sandwiches and chips. We _____ away all our trash. When we got home, I _____ out the candles on my birthday cake. I wished that I could go on another hike for my birthday next year!

Love,
Sue

Circle the correct word for each phrase.

What I Got for My Birthday:

1. Summer beach **clothes / close**
2. A **read / red** hat
3. A stuffed animal **bare / bear**
4. A **new / knew** backpack
5. A **pear / pair** of jeans

Times by 3

Multiply. Use the number words to write the answers in the puzzle.

ACROSS

2. 3 × 10 = _____

4. 3 × 4 = _____

6. 3 × 6 = _____

7. 3 × 1 = _____

8. 3 × 5 = _____

10. 3 × 2 = _____

11. 3 × 11 = _____

DOWN

1. 3 × 9 = _____

3. 3 × 7 = _____

4. 3 × 8 = _____

5. 3 × 12 = _____

9. 3 × 3 = _____

You're Invited!

You're having a summer swim party! Who will you invite?
What food will you serve? What games will you play?
List the items you will need below. Then make a party invitation.

FRIENDS TO INVITE

_____
_____
_____
_____
_____
_____

THINGS I NEED

_____
_____
_____
_____
_____
_____

FOOD

_____
_____
_____
_____
_____
_____

GAMES

_____
_____
_____
_____
_____
_____

It's a Swim Party!

Given by:

Where:

Date:

Time:

Make sure to bring:

RSVP by:

My phone number:

Rock and Roll Reading

Use the information below to the answer the questions.

Listen Up! All about Rock and Roll Music

Contents

1. In which chapter would you look to find information about drums and guitars? _3_

2. In which chapter would you look to learn more about rock music of the past? _____

3. Which chapter would have information about music that is popular now? _____

4. Which chapter is the longest one in the book? _____

5. If you turned to page 28, you might find information about

   a) the birth of rock music in America

   b) important rock groups

   c) rock music from the 1950s

   d) electric guitars

6. What type of book do you think this is?

   a) fiction

   b) nonfiction

   c) poetry

   d) a book of songs

7. Based on the book's title and table of contents, predict what you think the book will

   be about. _____

Good Timing

Look at each clock on the left. About what time is shown?
Draw a line to the closest time on the right.

midnight

nine fifteen

six forty-five

half past seven

four o'clock

one fifty

eleven o'clock

two twenty

Abbreviate It

Read the sentences. Then write the abbreviation for each underlined word.

	JUNE						
	SUN	MON	TUES	WED	THURS	FRI	SAT
				1	2	3	4
	5	6	7	8	9	10	11
	12	13	14	15	16	17	18
	19	20	21	22	23	24	25
	26	27	28	29	30		

1. School starts in <u>September</u>.

_____

2. <u>November</u> 12 is Dad's speech.

_____

3. Meet me <u>Sunday</u> morning.

_____

4. We got snow in <u>January</u>.

_____

5. <u>Mister</u> Shaw is our coach.

_____

6. Is the test on <u>Friday</u>?

_____

7. My vet is <u>Doctor</u> Wu.

_____

8. Mike <u>Senior</u> got a new job.

_____

9. The soccer game is on <u>Thursday</u>.

_____

10. <u>December</u> is the 12th month.

_____

11. I was born in <u>August</u>.

_____

12. I left early on <u>Wednesday</u>.

_____

13. James <u>Junior</u> scored the goal.

_____

14. Last <u>February</u> we moved.

_____

15. The store opens in <u>October</u>.

_____

16. I sleep in on <u>Saturday</u>.

_____

17. The field trip is <u>Tuesday</u>.

_____

18. Spring break is in <u>April</u>.

_____

19. <u>Missus</u> Banks is my teacher.

_____

20. <u>Monday</u> begins each week.

_____

Times Tables Targets

Multiply the number in the center of the target by each number around it. Write the answer.

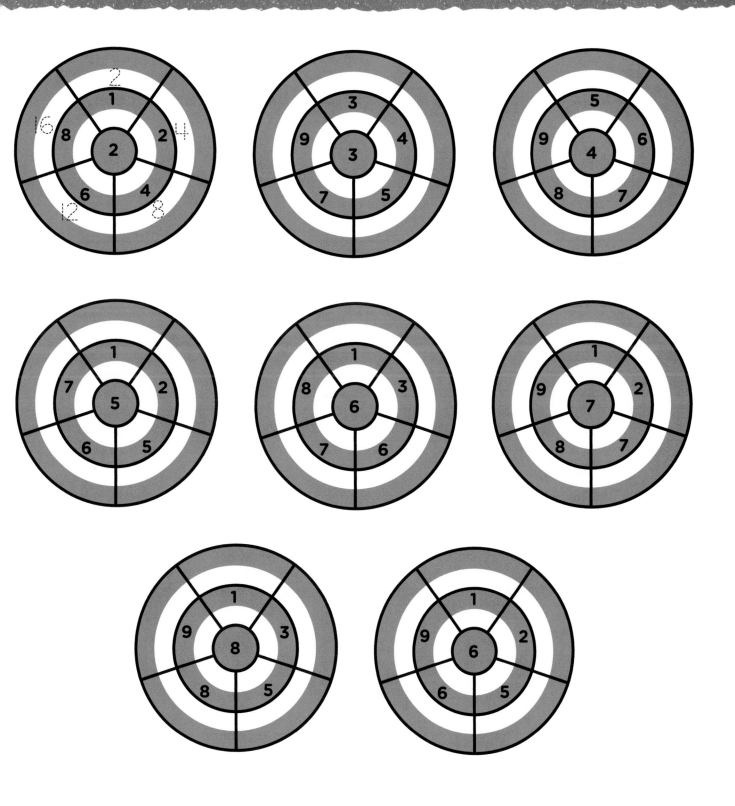

Times by 4

Multiply. Then "pop" the balloons by crossing off the answers.

4	4	4	4	4	4
× 12	× 9	× 1	× 7	× 11	× 4

4	4	4	4	4	4
× 10	× 8	× 2	× 6	× 3	× 5

Bunch 1

Bunch 2

Which bunch has the most balloons left? _____

Johnny Appleseed

Read the passage. Then answer the questions below.

John Chapman was born in Massachusetts in 1774. As he grew up, he learned to love nature. He loved hiking in the forest and swimming in the rivers near his home.

When John was 18 years old, he set out with a pack on his back and walked until he reached Pennsylvania in 1797. There, he decided to plant some apple seeds that were stored in his pack.

John traveled from place to place. He cleared spots of land and planted his apple seeds. He built fences around these orchards to keep them safe from animals. He did not want the animals to nibble on the small, tender plants.

Years later, John returned to check on his apple orchards. He found that they contained small trees. His trees were used for shade, and the apples they grew were used for cider. And that is how John Chapman got his nickname—Johnny Appleseed!

1. How old was John when he left Massachusetts? _____

2. What activities did John enjoy growing up? _____

3. When did John arrive in Pennsylvania? _____

4. How did he protect his trees from animals? _____

5. What did John find when he checked on his apple gardens? _____

_____

Bright Ideas

Each sentence below matches a picture. Copy each sentence beneath the picture that matches it.

Sunlight can be blocked to create shadows.

Light travels in a straight line.

Light is reflected from mirrors and other surfaces.

Sunlight contains all the colors of the rainbow.

1.

Light is reflected from
mirrors and other surfaces.

2.

_____

_____

3.

_____

_____

4.

_____

_____

Adding On

Follow the directions below.

A **prefix** is a word part added to the beginning of a word. Write the correct prefix to complete each word.

un + safe = unsafe

un = not	full = full of
re = again	dis = not
less = without	er = one who

1. My dinner got cold, so I need to ___re___ heat it.
2. When my best friend moved away, I felt _____ happy.
3. I need to _____ view the book again before the test.
4. I use my key to _____ lock the door.
5. I _____ like lemons because they are too sour!
6. When I broke my leg I was _____ able to run.
7. I spelled the word wrong, so I had to _____ write it.
8. I always argue and _____ agree with my sister.
9. The magician made the rabbit _____ appear.

A **suffix** is a word part added to the end of a word. Look at each word and its suffix, then match each word to its correct meaning.

10. joyful
11. useless
12. singer
13. painter
14. painful
15. harmless
16. fearless
17. careful
18. teacher

a) person who teaches
b) without fear
c) full of pain
d) without harm
e) full of joy
f) without use
g) a person who sings
h) full of care
i) a person who paints

Counting Coins

Read the word problems. Write how many quarters, dimes, nickels, and pennies equal the amount of money shown.

1. Jared has $1.35 in his pocket. He has 8 coins.

   _____ quarters
   _____ dimes
   _____ nickels
   _____ pennies

2. Jamie bought a soda for $1.32. He paid with 10 coins.

   _____ quarters
   _____ dimes
   _____ nickels
   _____ pennies

3. Kylie found $2.10 in the couch. She found 10 coins.

   _____ quarters
   _____ dimes
   _____ nickels
   _____ pennies

4. Torey has $3.25 for lunch. She has 2 one-dollar bills and 8 coins.

   _____ quarters
   _____ dimes
   _____ nickels
   _____ pennies

5. Lin gave the cashier $1.73. She gave him 12 coins.

   _____ quarters
   _____ dimes
   _____ nickels
   _____ pennies

6. Ben counted 8 coins in his desk. They added up to 41¢.

   _____ quarters
   _____ dimes
   _____ nickels
   _____ pennies

7. Mona paid 85¢ for an ice cream cone. She paid with 7 coins.

   _____ quarters
   _____ dimes
   _____ nickels
   _____ pennies

8. Wyatt grabbed 8 coins from his bank. They added up to 62¢.

   _____ quarters
   _____ dimes
   _____ nickels
   _____ pennies

All Aboard Arithmetic

Write the missing numbers to complete each equation.

Commutative Property
Numbers can be multiplied in any order and the product will remain the same!

1. **4 × 3 = 12**   **3 × 4 = 12**

    __4__ × __3__ = __3__ × __4__

2. **5 × 2 =___**   ___ × ___ = 10

    _____ × _____ = _____ × _____

3. **7 × 5 =___**   ___ × ___ = 35

    _____ × _____ = _____ × _____

4. **6 × ___ = 24**   ___ × ___ = ___

    _____ × _____ = _____ × _____

5. **___ × 8 = 56**   ___ × ___ = ___

    _____ × _____ = _____ × _____

6. **9 × ___ = 27**   ___ × ___ = ___

    _____ × _____ = _____ × _____

Times by 5

Multiply. Then write the answers on the lines using number words.

1. 5	2. 5	3. 5	4. 5	5. 5	6. 5
× 2	× 12	× 6	× 3	× 10	× 8

7. 5	8. 5	9. 5	10. 5	11. 5	12. 5
× 11	× 7	× 4	× 1	× 9	× 5

1. ◯ ____ ____
2. ____ ____ ____ ____ ____
3. ____ ◯ ____ ____ ____
4. ____ ____ ____ ____ ____ ◯ ____
5. ____ ____ ____ ____
6. ____ ____ ____ ____
7. ____ ____ ____ – ____ ____ ____ ◯
8. ____ ____ ____ ____ – ____ ____ ____ ____
9. ◯ ____ ____ ____ ____
10. ____ ____ ____ ◯ ____
11. ____ ◯ ____ ____ – ____ ____ ____ ____
12. ____ ____ ____ ____ ____ – ____ ____ ____ ◯

To solve the riddle, write the circled letters in order on the lines.

It happens once in a minute, twice in a week, and once in a year. What is it?

____ ____ ____   L____ ____ ____ ____ ____   ____

Dictionary Guide Words

Complete the activity below.

Do you know how to find words in a dictionary? They are listed in alphabetical order. Two words appear at the top of each page. They are called **guide words**.
- The first guide word is the first word on the page.
- The second guide word is the last word on the page.

Look at the guide words on each page. Then circle the words that would appear on that page.

1.

shine	*slant*	*wall*	*west*
shave		wallet	
silent		wiggle	
slow		wet	

2.

cook	*creak*	*meat*	*might*
coat		mile	
clean		meeting	
crane		must	

3.

jeep	*joke*	*black*	*book*
join		boring	
joy		bleed	
jail		break	

4.

sleep	*snore*	*peas*	*please*
story		pilot	
sneeze		pretty	
soup		peach	

5.

ace	*age*	*high*	*hope*
always		heal	
ache		hit	
apple		horse	

6.

eaten	*egg*	*rhino*	*right*
enter		roll	
eel		rubber	
eager		ride	

7.

veil	*violet*	*door*	*dream*
vein		deer	
vase		down	
vocal		dry	

8.

gleam	*grape*	*off*	*olive*
great		offer	
goat		over	
ghost		open	

Watch the Signs!

Complete each sentence by writing a **multiplication** or **division** sign on the line.

1.
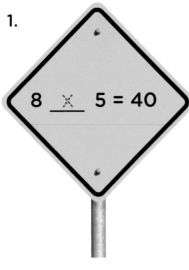
8 __×__ 5 = 40

2.
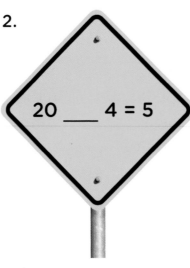
20 ___ 4 = 5

3.
5 ___ 5 = 1

4.
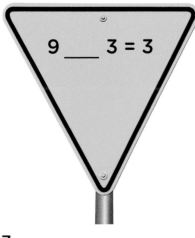
9 ___ 3 = 3

5.
10 ___ 2 = 20

6.

36 ___ 6 = 6

7.
3 ___ 4 = 12

8.

24 ___ 6 = 4

Travel Time

Read the passage and complete the activity below.

Think about the last time you traveled far from your home. How did you get there? You probably rode in a car, subway, train, or an airplane. Imagine what life was like when people didn't have these modes of transportation.

Long ago, people used horses for traveling long distances. People would ride on a horse's back or have the horses pull a wagon or carriage. If you needed to travel a long distance, you would probably go in a horse-drawn stagecoach. In a stagecoach it would take 24 hours to go 100 miles. If you were traveling from Los Angeles to New York City in a stagecoach, it would take about a month!

Today, we have trains that go 100 miles an hour and airplanes that go 550 miles an hour. Getting from Los Angeles to New York City only takes about six hours. Traveling long distances is easy and fast, so people do it all the time. In fact, Americans take about 2.6 billion long-distance trips every year!

If the sentence is about transportation in the past, circle **then**. If it's about transportation today, circle **now**.

1. Trains travel 100 miles an hour.   **then** **(now)**

2. Traveling from Los Angeles to New York City takes a month.   **then** **now**

3. Americans take 2.6 billion long-distance trips every year.   **then** **now**

4. People can take cars, subways, trains, or airplanes.   **then** **now**

5. Traveling from Los Angeles to New York City takes six hours.   **then** **now**

6. People ride in a horse-drawn wagon or carriage.   **then** **now**

Shifting Shapes

Shapes can be moved in different ways. The shape doesn't change, but it looks different. Follow the directions below.

1. Look at this shape. If you turn it upside down, what will it look like?

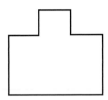

2. Look at this shape. If you turn it once to the right, what will it look like?

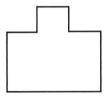

3. Look at this shape. How many surfaces does it have? _____

4. Look at this shape. How many surfaces does it have? _____

5. Look at this shape. How many surfaces does it have? _____

6. Look at this shape. How many surfaces does it have? _____

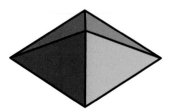

Best Friends

Read the passage. Then answer the questions.

In December 2004, a baby hippo was lost in the Indian Ocean. How did it get there? Giant waves had hit the coast of Africa. Some think heavy rains swept the baby and its herd down a river. But the baby was alone. The herd was nowhere to be seen.

Wildlife rangers found the baby hippo on the coast. It was weak and hungry. The rangers took it to Haller Park Animal Center. They named it Owen. They noticed that Owen seemed sad and lonely. "He probably misses his mother," a Haller Park ranger said.

Owen made a special friend at Haller Park—a giant male tortoise named Mzee. Owen found Mzee in the first couple of days. This may have happened because Mzee is big and gray like a hippo. No matter the reason, they liked each other right away.

Today Owen is doing great! Rangers say that Owen and Mzee are together all the time. They sleep, swim, and eat together. Owen follows Mzee around like a child. Owen needed a mother and apparently found one in Mzee!

1. How did Owen end up in the ocean? _____

_____

2. Who found Owen? _____

3. Where did they take Owen? _____

4. Who is Mzee? _____

5. Why do rangers think Owen likes Mzee? _____

_____

Creature Features

Each riddle below describes one animal's special features.
Solve each riddle and write the name of the animal on the line.

porcupine   skunk

koala   polar bear

turtle   elephant

1. I have thick white fur. My fur helps me blend in with the snow and keeps

   me warm. ___polar bear_____

2. I have very sharp claws for gripping tree branches. I can climb high up into a

   tree and escape! _____

3. I have a heavy shell around my body. I can pull my head and limbs inside the

   shell to hide. _____

4. I have sharp needles called quills on my skin. My quills help protect me from

   other animals. _____

5. If I lift up my tail, I can give off a stinky odor! This helps keep enemies away.

   _____

6. I have a long trunk that looks like a hose. I can use it to drink or to spray water

   on myself! _____

Look It Up!

Use the dictionary entries below to answer the questions.

bid | blame

big *a.* large, great.

bill[1] *n.* a bird's beak.

bill[2] *n.* a note of charges.

    v. to charge someone for a product or service.

bin *n.* a container for storing.

bis-cuit *n.* soft bread or a small cake.

bite *v.* to cut into something with your teeth.

    n. the act of biting; a mouthful.

bit-ter *a.* harsh-tasting, sharp.

1. Which words are adjectives? _____ , _____

2. Which word has two different meanings? _____
   Write a sentence for each word meaning.

   _____

   _____

3. Which two words have both a noun and a verb form? _____ ,

   _____

4. Which words have two syllables? _____ , _____

5. What are the guide words? _____ , _____

6. If you wanted to add the word **bird**, which two words on the page would
   you put it between? _____ and _____

7. Use the word **bite** in two sentences, once as a verb and once as a noun.

   _____

   _____

8. Which of the words below could appear on this dictionary page?
   Circle all the words.

birth	bet	bib	blade
black	blind	bike	blink

Times by 6

Multiply. Then gather acorns by circling the answers.

6 × 10	6 × 2	6 × 6	6 × 4	6 × 11	6 × 9

6 × 3	6 × 8	6 × 12	6 × 7	6 × 1	6 × 5

How many acorns did you gather?

_____

Kinds of Sentences

Complete the activity below.

A **telling** sentence makes a statement. It ends with a period. (**.**)
A **command** tells someone to do something. It ends with a period. (**.**)
An **asking** sentence asks a question. It ends with a question mark. (**?**)
An **exclamation** shows strong feeling. It ends with an exclamation point. (**!**)

Add the correct punctuation to each sentence. Then write **T** for **telling**, **C** for **command**, **A** for **asking**, and **E** for **exclamation**.

1. Whales are not fish; they are mammals ____ _____

2. Pet the dolphins gently ____ _____

3. What kind of food do crabs eat ____ _____

4. Don't touch anything in the tide pools ____ _____

5. Wow, that starfish grew a new leg ____ _____

6. Sharks do not have any bones in their bodies ____ _____

7. Do whales lay eggs or have live babies ____ _____

8. Ouch, that shark tooth is sharp ____ _____

Now, write sentences of your own.

Statement: _____

Command: _____

Asking: _____

Exclamation: _____

A Sea of Sentences

Read the paragraph. Then answer the questions.

(1) Jellyfish may look graceful as they drift in the ocean, but they can have quite a sting! (2) The sting comes from their long tentacles. (3) The tentacles of a jellyfish carry poison. (4) The smallest jellyfish is about 1 inch long. (5) Jellyfish use their tentacles to capture food. (6) When the tentacles touch another animal, they shoot poison into the victim. (7) Sometimes, jellyfish mistake humans for food and they sting a passing swimmer. (8) Swimming in the ocean is not safe when the water is too rough. (9) Although all jellyfish have tentacles that sting, the sting isn't always harmful to humans. (10) In fact, of the 2,000 species of jellyfish, only 70 have a sting that is harmful to humans. (11) Even if a jellyfish has washed up on the shore, its tentacles can still sting. (12) So you can look at a jellyfish, but don't touch!

1. Which sentence is the topic sentence? # _____

2. What is the topic of the paragraph? _____

3. There are two sentences that don't help support the topic sentence. Which sentences don't belong in the paragraph? # _____ and # _____

4. Which sentence explains how many species of jellyfish are harmful to humans? # _____

5. If you wanted to add some information to this paragraph, you could add details about

   a) which species of jellyfish are in the Atlantic Ocean

   b) the best aquariums where you can see jellyfish

   c) how it feels to be stung by a jellyfish

Frosty Fractions

Follow the directions below.

Look at the fraction inside each cone.
Find the scoop of ice cream with the equivalent fraction and circle it.

1. $\frac{2}{8}$ $\frac{6}{8}$ $\frac{3}{4}$

2. $\frac{4}{9}$ $\frac{4}{6}$ $\frac{2}{3}$

3. $\frac{2}{10}$ $\frac{2}{8}$ $\frac{1}{5}$

4. $\frac{3}{4}$ $\frac{3}{6}$ $\frac{1}{2}$

5. $\frac{2}{8}$ $\frac{4}{8}$ $\frac{1}{4}$

6.  $\frac{3}{9}$ $\frac{3}{6}$ $\frac{1}{3}$

7. $\frac{4}{50}$ $\frac{4}{10}$ $\frac{2}{5}$

8. $\frac{3}{16}$ $\frac{2}{12}$ $\frac{1}{6}$

| A **proper fraction** has a top number (numerator) that is lower than the bottom number (denominator). $\frac{3}{4}$ | An **improper fraction** has a numerator that is higher than its denominator. $\frac{5}{4}$ |

If the fraction is a proper fraction, write a
P inside the cone. If it the fraction is improper, write an **I**.

9.  $\frac{4}{3}$ I

10. $\frac{5}{6}$

11. $\frac{7}{4}$

12. $\frac{7}{8}$

13.  $\frac{2}{3}$

Shape Crossword

Look at each shape. Find its name in the box. Then write it in the puzzle.

| pentagon | triangle | octagon | diamond |
| oval | pyramid | cylinder | |

ACROSS

2.

7.

6.

DOWN

1.

3.

4.

5.

Correcting Sentences

Read each sentence. Then rewrite it correctly on the line.

- Add capital letters.
- Add commas (,) and quotation marks (" ").
- Add ending punctuation. (, ? !).

1. i got a job at the animal shelter jenny said

_____

2. the caring friends animal shelter is in shasta park

_____

3. how many people work at the shelter dad asked

_____

4. caring friends hires new workers in january and june

_____

5. the shelter takes in cats dogs rabbits snakes and birds

_____

6. mia has worked at caring friends since may 11 2002

_____

7. dr brown works there on mondays fridays and saturdays

_____

8. carlos has been missing his dog max since the fourth of july

_____

9. carlos asked do you think max might be at the shelter

_____

10. the gomez family finally found max on labor day

_____

Fraction Action

Fractions can be written as decimals. Draw a line to match each picture with the equivalent fraction and decimal.

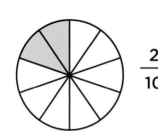

$$\frac{2}{10} = .2$$

1.
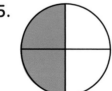

2.
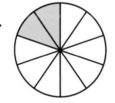

3.

4.

5.
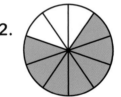

6.
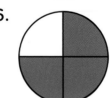

$$\frac{2}{10}$$

$$\frac{7}{10}$$

$$\frac{3}{10}$$

$$\frac{1}{4} = \frac{25}{100}$$

$$\frac{3}{4} = \frac{75}{100}$$

$$\frac{2}{4} = \frac{50}{100}$$

.7

.3

.2

.75

.50

.25

Flag Day

Read the passage. Then answer the questions.

The first settlers to live in America didn't have a flag. The American colonies were ruled by Great Britain, so people flew the British flag. George Washington decided that the United States needed its own flag because it was a new country. At this time, there were thirteen different colonies. So, the flag had thirteen stripes and thirteen stars to represent these colonies. Historians believe Betsy Ross designed the flag.

As the United States continued to grow, the look of the flag changed. Each time there was a new state, another star was added to the flag. The most recent star was added in 1959 when Hawaii became a state. The number of stripes has always remained at thirteen, in honor of the thirteen colonies.

The American flag is so special that there is a holiday in honor of it. A schoolteacher named B.J. Cigrand wanted a day for students to observe the birthday of the flag. On June 14 in 1885, he planned the first birthday celebration for the flag. The idea caught on with other teachers and kids, and after many years, Flag Day became a holiday!

1. Why did the United States need a new flag?
   a) The old flag belonged to Great Britain.
   b) America had gained its freedom from England and needed its own flag.
   c) There were thirteen new colonies.
2. What do the stripes on the flag represent?
   a) The thirteen stripes represent the thirteen original colonies.
   b) The thirteen stripes represent the US Continental Congress.
   c) There are fifty stripes on the flag to represent the fifty states.
3. How did Flag Day become a holiday?
   a) The Continental Congress declared Flag Day a holiday in 1777.
   b) People started celebrating Flag Day when Hawaii became a state in 1959.
   c) In 1885, a schoolteacher named B.J. Cigrand and his students celebrated the flag's birthday.
4. Put these events in order by numbering them from 1 to 4.
   a) _____ The Continental Congress agreed on the official design of the flag.
   b) _____ Hawaii became a state and another star was added to the flag.
   c) _____ The thirteen colonies flew the British flag.
   d) _____ B.J. Cigrand and his students celebrated the first "Flag Birthday."

Times by 7

Multiply. Use the answers to find your way to the seeds in the center of the apple. An answer may appear on the path more than once.

$$\begin{array}{r} 7 \\ \times\ 6 \\ \hline \end{array} \qquad \begin{array}{r} 7 \\ \times\ 1 \\ \hline \end{array} \qquad \begin{array}{r} 7 \\ \times\ 12 \\ \hline \end{array} \qquad \begin{array}{r} 7 \\ \times\ 10 \\ \hline \end{array} \qquad \begin{array}{r} 7 \\ \times\ 8 \\ \hline \end{array} \qquad \begin{array}{r} 7 \\ \times\ 4 \\ \hline \end{array}$$

$$\begin{array}{r} 7 \\ \times\ 9 \\ \hline \end{array} \qquad \begin{array}{r} 7 \\ \times\ 5 \\ \hline \end{array} \qquad \begin{array}{r} 7 \\ \times\ 3 \\ \hline \end{array} \qquad \begin{array}{r} 7 \\ \times\ 11 \\ \hline \end{array} \qquad \begin{array}{r} 7 \\ \times\ 2 \\ \hline \end{array} \qquad \begin{array}{r} 7 \\ \times\ 7 \\ \hline \end{array}$$

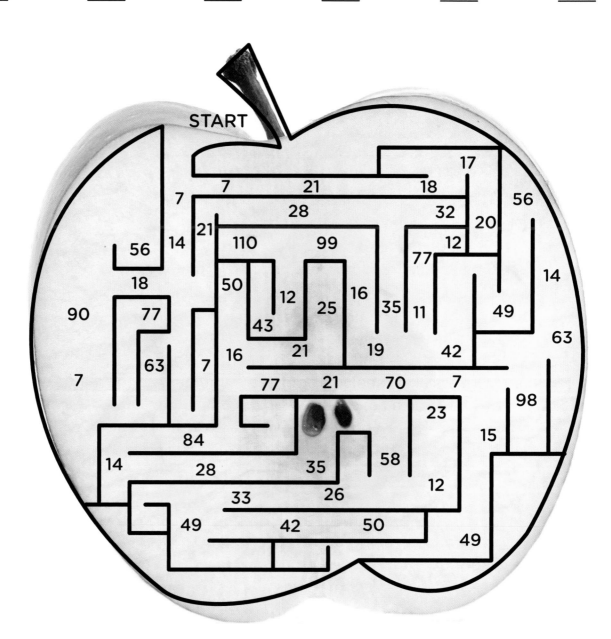

Recording Rainfall

A **biome** is a community of plants and animals. Each of the biomes listed below has a different climate. This graph shows the average inches of rain each of these biomes receives in a year.

inches of rain	TUNDRA	GRASSLAND	FOREST	RAINFOREST	DESERT
90					
80					
70					
60					
50					
40					
30					
20					
10					

Write **true** or **false** for each statement below.

1. A tundra receives more rain than a desert. _____false_____

2. A rainforest receives the most rain. _____

3. A tundra and a grassland receive about the same amount of rainfall. _____

4. A forest receives about twice as much rain as a grassland. _____

5. There is no rainfall in a desert. _____

6. A tundra and a desert receive the least amount of rainfall. _____

A Walk Down Word Lane

Complete the activity below.

A **synonym** is a word that means the same thing as another word. Match each word with its synonym.

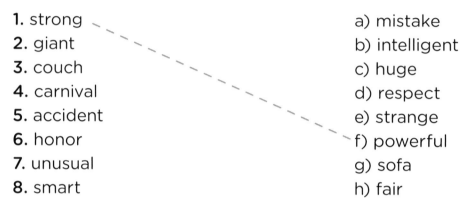

1. strong
2. giant
3. couch
4. carnival
5. accident
6. honor
7. unusual
8. smart

a) mistake
b) intelligent
c) huge
d) respect
e) strange
f) powerful
g) sofa
h) fair

An **antonym** is a word that means the opposite of another word. The pairs of words below are antonyms. Find the pair of words that completes each sentence and write the correct word in each blank.

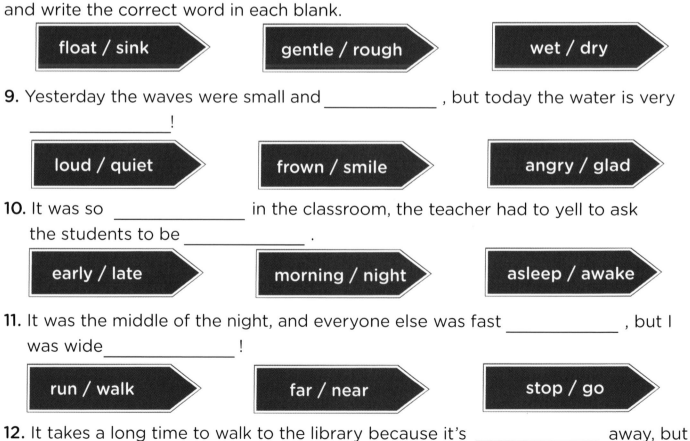

> float / sink

> gentle / rough

> wet / dry

9. Yesterday the waves were small and _____ , but today the water is very _____!

> loud / quiet

> frown / smile

> angry / glad

10. It was so _____ in the classroom, the teacher had to yell to ask the students to be _____ .

> early / late

> morning / night

> asleep / awake

11. It was the middle of the night, and everyone else was fast _____ , but I was wide_____!

> run / walk

> far / near

> stop / go

12. It takes a long time to walk to the library because it's _____ away, but the school is very _____!

Star Power

Multiply. Then tell if the first product is **less than**, **greater than**, or **equal to** the second product by writing **<**, **>**, or **=** in the star.

1. 5 × 5 ⭐ 9 × 3

2. 6 × 9 ⭐ 4 × 12

3. 2 × 4 ⭐ 1 × 6

4. 5 × 6 ⭐ 10 × 3

5. 8 × 7 ⭐ 5 × 9

6. 4 × 4 ⭐ 7 × 2

7. 11 × 3 ⭐ 6 × 6

8. 9 × 9 ⭐ 8 × 11

9. 5 × 8 ⭐ 4 × 10

10. 10 × 2 ⭐ 4 × 5

11. 3 × 6 ⭐ 9 × 2

12. 10 × 3 ⭐ 6 × 4

13. 7 × 7 ⭐ 8 × 6

14. 12 × 2 ⭐ 7 × 4

15. 1 × 9 ⭐ 3 × 3

16. 10 × 10 ⭐ 12 × 9

Word Play

How many smaller words can you find in this larger word? Hint: No plurals are allowed!

STARFISH

TWO LETTERS

_____   _____

_____   _____

_____

THREE LETTERS

_____   _____   _____

_____   _____   _____

_____   _____   _____

_____   _____   _____

FOUR LETTERS

_____   _____   _____

_____   _____   _____

_____   _____   _____

FIVE LETTERS

_____   _____

_____   _____

Camp Comma

Read the passage below. Insert commas where they are needed.

Use commas to separate
The day, month, and year: *Wednesday, June 21, 1995*
The city and state: *Chicago, Illinois*
Items in a list: *apples, oranges, and berries*

If you want to have a great summer, spend a week at our camp in Portland Oregon. The first day of camp this year is Saturday June 30. Camp runs all summer until Wednesday August 15.

People have been coming to Camp Comma for years! A small campground was opened here on June 1 1955. People came to enjoy the hiking waterfalls and fishing. Then, on April 20, 1980, Carl Comma decided to open a camp for kids. Now kids come from all over the country to enjoy Camp Comma. We have kids from San Diego California, and even Fairbanks Alaska.

When you come to Camp Comma, don't forget to bring a sleeping bag a flashlight and a bathing suit.

The deadline to enroll for camp is Friday April 26. Don't wait!

Times by 8

Multiply. Circle the cones that have the answers to help Cassie get through the skating maze.

8 × 1	8 × 6	8 × 11	8 × 7	8 × 2	8 × 5

8 × 9	8 × 8	8 × 3	8 × 10	8 × 4	8 × 12

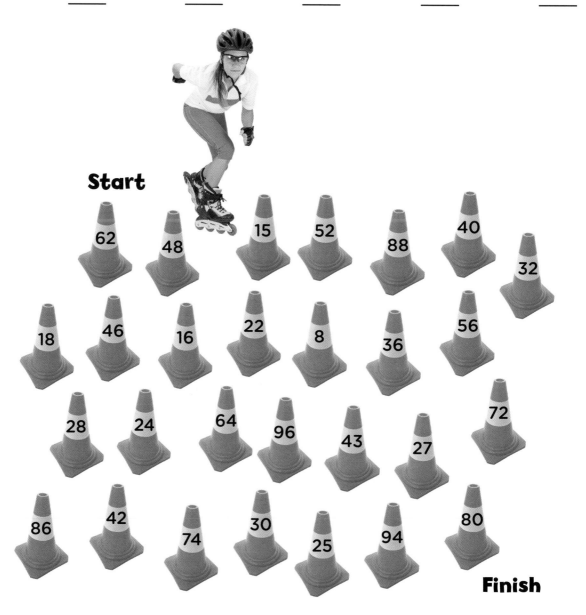

Start

62 48 15 52 88 40 32

18 46 16 22 8 36 56

28 24 64 96 43 27 72

86 42 74 30 25 94 80

Finish

Making Contractions

Complete the activity below.

A **contraction** is a word formed by combining two words and leaving out some letters or sounds. For example, *can't* is a contraction of the words *can* and *not*. Make contractions by adding the following words together. Write the new words on the line.

1. did + not = _____

2. I + will = _____

3. we + will = _____

4. we + are = _____

5. I + am = _____

6. do + not = _____

7. you + are = _____

8. they + are = _____

9. they + will = _____

10. he + is = _____

11. will + not = _____

12. she + will = _____

Write the contraction for each pair of words in ( ). Write it on the line.

13. (We are) building a sand castle on the seashore.   _____

14. Brett says (he will) make a moat around it to catch water.   _____

15. I (did not) see the big wave coming toward us.   _____

16. Oh, no! Now (we will) have to start all over again!   _____

Ship Shape

Write the name of each four-sided shape.

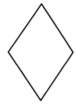 A **rhombus** has four parallel sides of equal length.

 A **parallelogram** has four sides, and opposite sides are parallel.

 A **rectangle** has four right angles.

 A **square** has four right angles, and all sides are the same length.

1.

rectangle

2.

_____

3.

_____

4.

_____

5.

_____

6.

_____

What's in a Name?

Many of our states' names come from Native American words.
Match each state with its Native American origin. Look for words that sound
similar to the name of the state. Then write the matching letter next to each state.

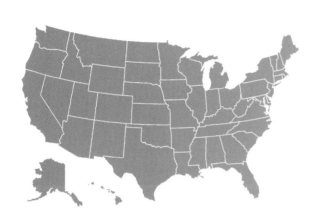

1. Texas _____

2. Tennessee _____

3. Mississippi _____

4. Indiana _____

5. Hawaii _____

6. Illinois _____

7. Alabama _____

8. Alaska _____

a) Named after *Tanasia*, a Cherokee Village

b) From the word *Hawaiki*, which means "homeland"

c) Called Land of the *Indians*

d) From the word *alakshak*, which means "great lands"

e) Named after a tribe called the *Alibamu*

f) From the word *iliniwek*, which means "warriors"

g) From the word *messipi*, which means "great river"

h) From the word *tejas*, which means "allies"

Graph It!

How many arms does a crab have? Follow the directions below.
The answer will appear in the graph! Hint: the first
number in each coordinate is from the top of the graph.

Draw a colored dot on each coordinate:

1. Blue (4,6)

4. Blue (4,5)

7. Blue (4,3)

10. Red (7,3)

13. Blue (4,4)

2. Red (9,4)

5. Red (8,3)

8. Blue (4,7)

11. Red (6,6)

14. Red (9,5)

3. Red (7,7)

6. Red (6,5)

9. Red (9,6)

12. Red (8,7)

15. Red (6,4)

Draw a blue line to connect the blue dots.
Draw a red line to connect the red dots.

Answer: A crab has _____ arms.

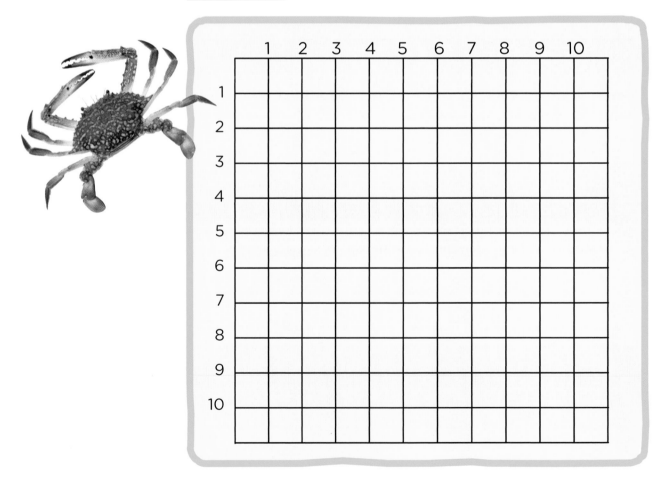

Awesome Ads

Read the ad below. Then answer the questions.

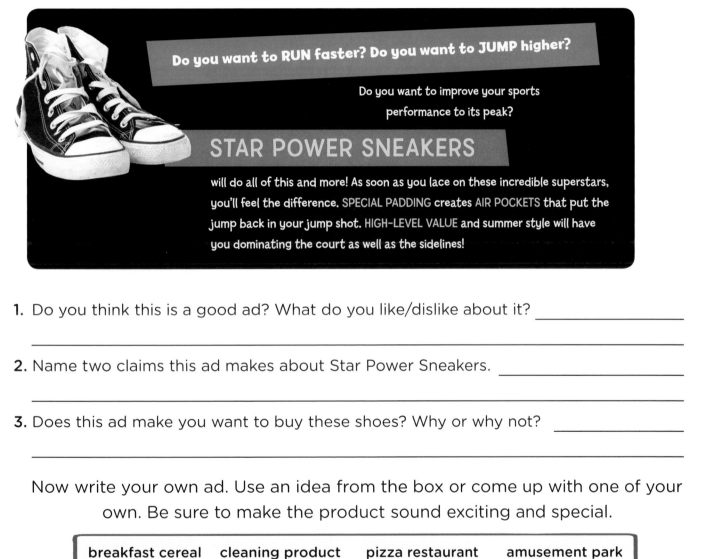

Do you want to RUN faster? Do you want to JUMP higher?

Do you want to improve your sports performance to its peak?

STAR POWER SNEAKERS

will do all of this and more! As soon as you lace on these incredible superstars, you'll feel the difference. SPECIAL PADDING creates AIR POCKETS that put the jump back in your jump shot. HIGH-LEVEL VALUE and summer style will have you dominating the court as well as the sidelines!

1. Do you think this is a good ad? What do you like/dislike about it? _____

_____

2. Name two claims this ad makes about Star Power Sneakers. _____

_____

3. Does this ad make you want to buy these shoes? Why or why not? _____

_____

Now write your own ad. Use an idea from the box or come up with one of your own. Be sure to make the product sound exciting and special.

breakfast cereal	cleaning product	pizza restaurant	amusement park
jeans	dog treats	study aid	hair product

Moon Mysteries

Complete the activity below.

The shape of the moon looks a little different each night. That's because the moon is moving in an orbit around Earth. We see the moon from different angles as it reflects light from the sun. The moon passes through four main shapes, called the **phases of the moon**.

Read the description for each phase of the moon. Draw a line to match each description with the correct picture.

1. The moon, Earth, and sun are in a straight line, but the lighted side of the moon faces away from the Earth. So, the moon we see looks very dark.

a) Last Quarter

b) Full Moon

2. The left half of the moon is still dark, but the right half is lighted. The lighted parts get larger and larger each day.

3. Earth, the sun, and the moon are in a straight line, and the lighted side is facing Earth. The moon is a very bright full circle.

c) New Moon

4. The left half of the moon stays bright, but the right side is dark. The dark part of the moon grows larger every day.

d) First Quarter

Times by 9

Look at the symbol in each problem. Check the code to find the corresponding number. Then write out and solve the problem.

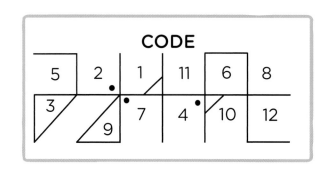

1. 9 × ⌊

   9 × ___ = ___

2. 9 × □

   9 × ___ = ___

3. 9 × ◹

   9 × ___ = ___

4. 9 × ⌐•

   9 × ___ = ___

5. 9 × ⌐

   9 × ___ = ___

6. 9 × ⌐|

   9 × ___ = ___

7. 9 × □

   9 × ___ = ___

8. 9 × •⌐

   9 × ___ = ___

9. 9 × ◿

   9 × ___ = ___

10. 9 × ⌊•

    9 × ___ = ___

11. 9 × ⌊◹

    9 × ___ = ___

12. 9 × ⌊⌋

    9 × ___ = ___

Syllable Search

Say each word aloud slowly. Write the number of syllables you hear on the line. Then draw a line to show the syllable parts.

Example: __2__ pan/da

1. _____ monkey

2. _____ flamingo

3. _____ zebra

4. _____ tiger

5. _____ elephant

6. _____ conservation

7. _____ zookeeper

8. _____ hyena

9. _____ lion

10. _____ rattlesnake

11. _____ wolf

12. _____ fox

13. _____ camel

14. _____ gorilla

15. _____ wilderness

16. _____ orangutan

17. _____ parrot

18. _____ giraffe

19. _____ kangaroo

20. _____ chimpanzee

Fran and Jan

Read the story. Then answer the questions.

Fran and Jan were twin sisters, so they looked the same. But they couldn't have been more different! Fran liked hiking outdoors and playing sports. Jan liked reading books and writing stories. When the family had to decide where to go on summer vacation, Fran and Jan disagreed.

"Let's go camping and hike to the top of a mountain!" said Fran.

"No way!" said Jan. "I want to read a book by the pool and go to museums."

Fran and Jan's parents suggested lots of vacation spots, but the girls just couldn't agree.

"Since you can't agree," said Fran's mother, "then we'll just have to split up!"

They decided that Fran and her mother would go camping in the mountains. Jan and her father would stay in a beach house.

For the first few days the girls had fun, but soon they started to miss each other. It wasn't really a family vacation if the whole family wasn't together! The family members decided that next year they would find a vacation spot that everyone would enjoy.

1. Why couldn't Fran and Jan agree on a place for the family vacation?
   a) Fran wanted to go somewhere far away, but Jan wanted to stay close to home.
   b) The sisters had different ideas about what they wanted to do.
   c) They didn't want to go anywhere together.

2. Why did Fran's mother decide they should split up?
   a) Fran's parents wanted to do different things.
   b) Fran and Jan didn't want to spend time together.
   c) Fran and Jan couldn't agree on where to go.

3. How did the girls feel at the end of the vacation?
   a) They were glad that they got to do what they wanted.
   b) They missed each other and felt lonely.
   c) They were angry at their parents.

4. Write some words that describe Fran:

_____

5. Write some words that describe Jan:

_____

6. Where do you think the family should go on vacation next year?

_____

Making Change

Look at the coin values below. Then solve the problems.

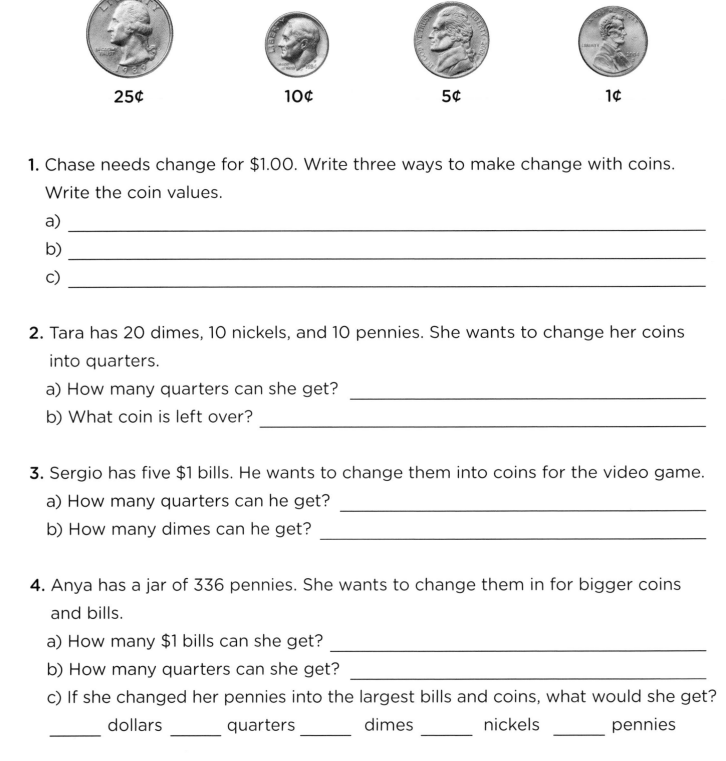

25¢   10¢   5¢   1¢

1. Chase needs change for $1.00. Write three ways to make change with coins.
   Write the coin values.

   a) _____

   b) _____

   c) _____

2. Tara has 20 dimes, 10 nickels, and 10 pennies. She wants to change her coins
   into quarters.
   a) How many quarters can she get? _____

   b) What coin is left over? _____

3. Sergio has five $1 bills. He wants to change them into coins for the video game.
   a) How many quarters can he get? _____

   b) How many dimes can he get? _____

4. Anya has a jar of 336 pennies. She wants to change them in for bigger coins
   and bills.
   a) How many $1 bills can she get? _____

   b) How many quarters can she get? _____

   c) If she changed her pennies into the largest bills and coins, what would she get?

   _____ dollars _____ quarters _____ dimes _____ nickels _____ pennies

Acrostic Poem

An acrostic poem is easy to write! Choose a topic, such as cats.
Then write a line that begins with each letter in the word.
Your poem does not have to rhyme.

Example:

Cuddling in my lap
Asking for milk with a gentle purr
Tiptoeing quietly through the grass
Sleeping in the warm sun

Now, write an acrostic poem about a vacation. It can be a vacation
you want to take or one you've been on before. Use the letters below.
Use your imagination!

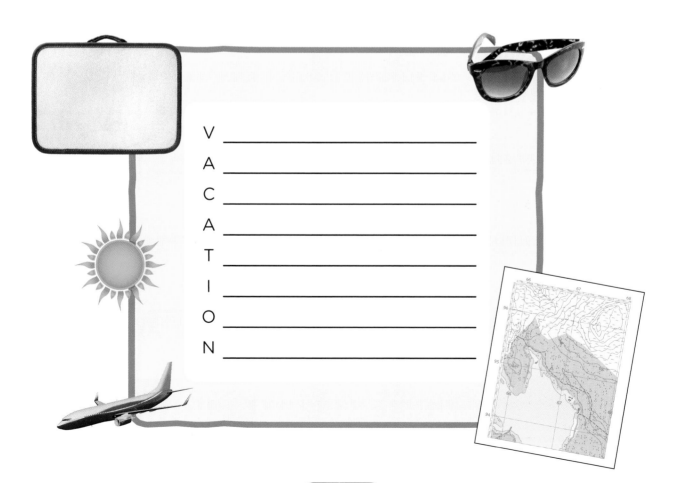

V _____

A _____

C _____

A _____

T _____

I _____

O _____

N _____

Shapes with Faces

Three-dimensional shapes have sides and edges. These sides are called **faces**.
Some faces are flat and some are curved. Count the number
of faces on each shape and fill in the chart below.

	SHAPES		FLAT FACES	CURVED FACES
1.	cube	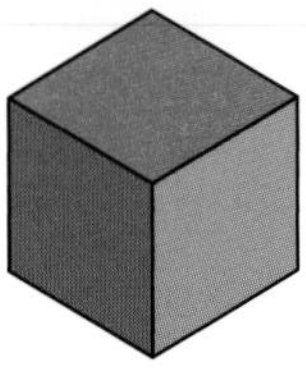	6	0
2.	pyramid	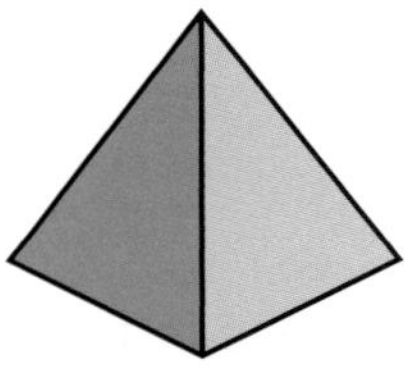		
3.	prism	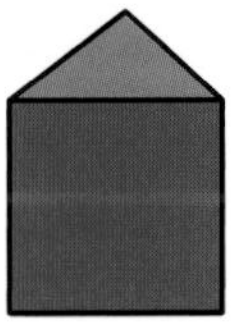		
4.	cone	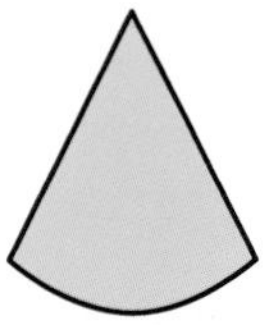		
5.	cylinder			
6.	sphere			

The President's Palace

Read the passage and follow the directions below.

Most people know that the White House is the place where the president of the United States lives. It's much more than just a home, however. It's also a workplace, a historical landmark, and an important American symbol.

George Washington had someone begin building what he called the President's Palace in 1792. It wasn't finished until 1800, so George Washington never actually lived in the White House! John Adams was the first president to live there. People nicknamed the house the White House because of its color, but it wasn't until 1901 that Theodore Roosevelt officially renamed it the White House.

The White House is a busy place and has different rooms for everything that goes on there. In fact, there are six floors in all, with a total of 132 rooms and 32 bathrooms! Only two floors are used for the president and his family to live in. The Oval Office is the president's office. He signs documents, meets with small groups of people, and makes telephone calls from the Oval Office. In the Cabinet Room, the president sits around a large table for debate and discussion with his staff. The Blue Room is a small room for greeting guests. The State Dining Room is a large room where 140 people can sit down to dinner.

People come from all over to visit the White House and tour some of the rooms. In fact, there are about 6,000 visitors a day!

Draw a line to match each word with its meaning.

1. cabinet

2. landmark

3. debate

4. documents

a) discussion between people with different opinions

b) important papers

c) a group of people chosen by a political leader

d) a historically important structure

Decide which room in the White House would be the best place for each event.

5. The president is sitting at his desk signing some papers.

_____

6. The president is discussing important issues with many members of his staff.

_____

7. Leaders from another country are coming to a dinner at the White House.

_____

8. A few visitors are coming to meet with the president on a social visit.

_____

Times by 10

Multiply. Use the number words to write the answers in the puzzle.

ACROSS

2. 10 × 8= _____

6. 10 × 9 = _____

8. 10 × 7 = _____

10. 10 × _____ = 120

11. 10 × _____ = 30

DOWN

1. 10 × 6 = _____

3. 10 × _____ = 100

4. 10 × 5 = _____

5. 10 × _____ = 10

7. 10 × 4 = _____

9. 10 × _____ = 110

11. 10 × 2 = _____

Messy Morgan

Read the story and complete the activity below.

Messy Morgan did not like to clean. Every day, the mess piled up in her room. Her parents were tired of nagging. "If you want to live in a mess, then go ahead," her mom said. "Just keep this door shut!" Messy Morgan was pleased. First, she threw her clothes on the floor. She wrote a book report, then threw crumpled paper on her clothes. Done with the pizza? There goes the pizza box!

She couldn't find her trash can anymore, so she threw a couple of banana peels onto the pile. Then she added empty soda cans and dirty paper plates. "What's next?" you might ask. Messy Morgan carelessly tossed on an old notebook, a broken yo-yo, a torn shirt, and some wilted lettuce from a half-eaten sandwich. By now, the stinky stack almost reached the ceiling. Before she knew it, Messy Morgan couldn't get out the door. She was trapped behind a tower of trash!

Can you help Messy Morgan clean her room?

In order, tell which items need to be thrown away. Remember, you're going from the top of the trash tower to the bottom.

1. _____

2. _____

3. _____

4. _____

5. _____

6. _____

7. _____

8. _____

9. _____

10. _____

Postcard from Another Planet

Read about Venus and think about how this planet compares to Earth.
Then pretend that you're visiting Venus, and write a
postcard home to tell your family about it.

- Venus is sometimes called Earth's "twin." That's because the two planets are similar in size and make up. Venus is Earth's closest neighbor, even though it is about 25 million miles away.
- The surface of Venus is covered in craters, mountains, volcanoes, and lava plains. There are no oceans on Venus.
- Venus is about 67 million miles away from the sun. The temperature on Venus is about 900 degrees Farenheit! In fact, it's the hottest place in the solar system after the sun.
- The highest point on Venus is Maxwell Montes. It's 7 miles high!
- Venus spins in the opposite direction of Earth. So the sun rises in the west and sets in the east.
- Venus is surrounded by thick clouds that reflect the sun's light. This makes Venus the brightest object in the sky after the sun and the moon.

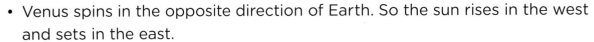

Dear Family,

I'm having a great time on Venus! So far I've seen _____
_____.

I like Venus because _____.

Venus is a lot like Earth because _____
_____.

Venus is also different from Earth because _____
_____.

I want to see _____ before I come home!

Sincerely,

_____

Let's All Agree!

Read each sentence. Underline the subject and circle the verb.
If the subject and the verb don't agree, rewrite the sentence below.
Can the kids agree on what type of pizza to order?

1. Tim and Bill likes lots of cheese.

2. Sally wants pepperoni and mushrooms.

3. Everyone get his or her own drink.

4. The waiter bring a big salad for everyone to share.

5. Bill want mushrooms on the pizza.

6. Tim and Sally get onions instead of mushrooms.

7. All the kids wants pepperoni.

8. Tim, Bill, and Sally order a pepperoni pizza with extra cheese.

Five are incorrect sentences. Rewrite each sentence
so the subject and verb agree.

_____

_____

_____

_____

_____

Summing It Up

Circle the two numbers in each grid that add up to the sum.

1.

103	213
225	170

SUM: 316

2.

612	336
310	505

SUM: 922

3.

445	622
391	608

SUM: 999

4.

175	410
312	205

SUM: 585

5.

417	327
445	290

SUM: 772

6.

225	260
208	275

SUM: 483

7.

323	340
284	296

SUM: 607

8.

121	399
407	231

SUM: 528

9.

110	127
116	103

SUM: 219

10.

185	398
190	446

SUM: 636

11.

918	885
372	476

SUM: 1,290

12.

518	463
487	509

SUM: 1,005

In Agreement

Follow the directions below.

Underline the **subject** in each sentence. Circle the **verb**. If the subject and the verb agree, write **yes** on the line. If the subject and the verb do not agree, change the verb to agree with the subject. Write the new sentence on the line.

1. Jerome have a very exciting and rewarding job.

   _____

2. He is a firefighter for the New York City Fire Department.

   _____

3. Firefighters not only puts out fires but also rescue people.

   _____

4. Ana finish school this year to become a veterinarian.

   _____

5. She will spends her time helping animals when they're sick.

   _____

6. Vets needs to go to school for a long time.

   _____

7. When I grows up, I want to be a detective!

   _____

8. Detectives look for clues in order to solve crimes.

   _____

9. Hair, fibers, and fingerprints is all good clues.

   _____

10. Do you knows anyone who works for the police force?

   _____

Lost Luggage

Erica can't find her luggage at the airport! Read the conversation between Erica and her Aunt Mary. Circle the correct word for each sentence.

Aunt Mary: I can't believe **your / you're** finally here!
⠀⠀⠀⠀⠀⠀⠀⠀⠀⠀⠀⠀⠀⠀⠀**1**

Erica: I can't wait to go to **your / you're** house and see my cousins.
⠀⠀⠀⠀⠀⠀⠀⠀⠀⠀⠀⠀⠀⠀⠀⠀**2**

Aunt Mary: Yes, **their / they're** very excited to see you!
⠀⠀⠀⠀⠀⠀⠀⠀⠀⠀⠀**3**

Erica: I need to get my luggage. It should be over **there / their**.
⠀⠀⠀⠀⠀⠀⠀⠀⠀⠀⠀⠀⠀⠀⠀⠀⠀⠀⠀⠀⠀**4**

Aunt Mary: Do you see **your / you're** bag yet?
⠀⠀⠀⠀⠀⠀⠀⠀⠀⠀⠀⠀⠀**5**

Erica: **There / They're** it is!
⠀⠀⠀⠀⠀⠀⠀**6**

Aunt Mary: Wait! That couple is going toward the bag. **Their / They're** picking it up!
⠀⠀⠀⠀⠀⠀⠀⠀⠀⠀⠀⠀⠀⠀⠀⠀⠀⠀⠀⠀⠀⠀⠀⠀⠀⠀⠀**7**

Erica: It must be **there / their** bag.
⠀⠀⠀⠀⠀⠀⠀⠀⠀**8**

Aunt Mary: Then where is **your / you're** bag?
⠀⠀⠀⠀⠀⠀⠀⠀⠀⠀⠀⠀⠀**9**

Erica: **There / Their** it is!
⠀⠀⠀⠀⠀⠀⠀**10**

Aunt Mary: Hey, here comes that couple. **Their / They're** walking right toward us.
⠀⠀⠀⠀⠀⠀⠀⠀⠀⠀⠀⠀⠀⠀⠀⠀⠀⠀⠀⠀**11**

Man: Excuse me, is this **your / you're** bag?
⠀⠀⠀⠀⠀⠀⠀⠀⠀⠀⠀⠀**12**

Erica: Yes! Thank you for bringing it to us. **Your / You're** very kind.
⠀⠀⠀⠀⠀⠀⠀⠀⠀⠀⠀⠀⠀⠀⠀⠀⠀⠀⠀⠀**13**

Woman: We made a mistake. I hope **you're / your** not too upset.
⠀⠀⠀⠀⠀⠀⠀⠀⠀⠀⠀⠀⠀⠀⠀⠀**14**

Aunt Mary: Erica, if they had **your / you're** bag, you must have **they're / their** bag!
⠀⠀⠀⠀⠀⠀⠀⠀⠀⠀⠀⠀⠀**15**⠀⠀⠀⠀⠀⠀⠀⠀⠀⠀⠀⠀⠀⠀⠀⠀**16**

Erica: Oops!

Times by 11

Multiply across, and then multiply down. If your answers
are correct, they will add up to the same sum.

Example:

11	7	77
3	11	33
33	77	(110)

1.

8	11	
11	11	
		◯

2.

11	9	
1	11	
		◯

3.

3	11	
11	5	
		◯

4.

11	12	
2	11	
		◯

5.

11	7	
4	11	
		◯

6.

11	9	
0	11	
		◯

7.

5	11	
11	6	
		◯

8.

10	11	
11	12	
		◯

9.

11	11	
4	11	
		◯

Said Is Dead!

Many words are used very often in the English language. A few of these are **said**, **happy**, **sad**, **hot**, **cold**, **mad**, **good**, **bad**, **big**, and **small**.

Look at the underlined word in each sentence.
Then write two interesting words you could use
in place of that word on the lines.

1. The <u>big</u> volcano rumbled, sending smoke and ash into the air.
   _____   _____

2. Jason gave the <u>small</u> mouse some cheese from his sandwich.
   _____   _____

3. We were <u>happy</u> that the blizzard was finally over.
   _____   _____

4. The <u>mad</u> tornado downed trees and tossed trash cans like toys.
   _____   _____

5. "Please help me with the dishes after dinner," Dad <u>said</u>.
   _____   _____

6. The crowd <u>yelled</u> as Wendy Wilcox scored another goal.
   _____   _____

7. <u>Cold</u> air filled the house as soon as he opened the door.
   _____   _____

8. Thunder <u>crashed</u> and lightning lit up the night sky.
   _____   _____

Now, rewrite each sentence below. Add at least
two interesting describing words to make the sentence better.

9. The horse galloped across the beach.
   _____

10. The baseball players surrounded their coach.
    _____

Summer Spree!

Complete each problem. Show your work.

$5.25

$8.50

$3.00

$4.75

$2.50

1. Jane bought 3 beach chairs. What was the total price?

$8.50 + $8.50 + $8.50 = $25.50

2. Kirk bought 4 beach towels. How much did he spend in all?

_____

3. Lucy spent $10.00 on flip-flops. How many pairs did she buy?

_____

4. Greg has $9.00 he wants to spend on beach balls. How many can he buy?

_____

5. Troy spent exactly $10.00 and he bought 2 items. Which 2 things did he buy?

_____

6. Martha bought a hat and a pair of flip-flops. How much did she spend in all?

_____

Ben Franklin

Read about the life of Ben Franklin. Then fill in the missing words and dates on the time line below.

Ben Franklin was a leader in almost every part of American life. Born in 1706 in Boston, Franklin loved reading and writing even as a young boy. He wanted everyone to enjoy books, so he started the first public library in 1731. Franklin was always thinking of new ideas to help people. Around 1742 he invented a heater called the Franklin Stove. This worked much better than a fireplace because it gave off more heat with less smoke and used less wood.

Franklin was a leader in education, and in 1751 he helped start the Academy of Philadelphia. This academy later became the University of Pennsylvania. Ben Franklin also played an important role in American politics. He helped write and signed the Declaration of Independence in 1776 and the US Constitution in 1787.

TIME LINE				
1706				
Ben Franklin was born in _____ .	Started the first public _____ .	Invented the _____ Stove.	Helped start the Academy of _____ .	Signed the _____ of _____ .

Division Puzzle

There are 16 division problems in this puzzle. Circle each problem.
Hint: Problems can go across or down. A number can
be used in more than one problem.

20	18	6	33	12	25	5	4
15	66	6	11	3	18	21	2
5	5	1	30	6	9	3	15
3	45	6	10	24	2	20	5
14	7	2	48	8	6	4	32
6	16	27	12	3	40	5	8
8	9	3	4	18	10	16	4
2	0	9	3	3	24	8	2

Experiment Time!

This graph shows the results of an experiment that was done with two plants. Read about the experiment and study the graph.

Procedure: Two plastic cups were filled with cotton and five wheat seeds. Cup A had no salt. In Cup B, some salt was added to the bottom of the cup. Both cups were kept moist with water and received plenty of light.

Observations:

	Cup A No Salt	**Cup B** Salt Added
Day 1:	The beans are swelling.	The beans look the same.
Day 2:	Two beans have sprouted.	There is no change.
Day 3:	The other three beans sprouted.	There is a slight swelling in two beans.
Day 4:	Stalks are growing from three beans.	Two beans have small sprouts.
Day 5:	Stalks are growing from all five beans.	A total of three beans have small sprouts. No stalks are growing.

Evidence is an outward fact or sign. An **opinion** is a personal belief or view. Read the sentences below. If the statement is a piece of evidence, write **E**. If the statement is an opinion, write **O**.

1. The beans in Cup A sprouted more quickly than those in Cup B. _____E_____

2. The stalks that grew in Cup A were pretty. _____

3. The beans in Cup A grew stalks within a few days. _____

4. The cups were too small to hold all the beans. _____

5. No stalks grew from the beans in Cup B. _____

6. Based on the experiment, which of the following is the most logical conclusion?
   a) Seeds planted in salty soil will grow much more quickly.
   b) Adding salt helps seeds to soak up more water.
   c) Seeds and plants do not grow as well when salt is present.

Stories with Sense

Details that appeal to the five senses help make a story more interesting.
Read the story. Find the details that appeal to each
of the five senses and write them on the lines below.

On the Fourth of July, I went with my family to a carnival.
As soon as we got there, I could smell hot dogs and
hamburgers cooking and sizzling on the grill. I bit into a
juicy slice of watermelon and enjoyed the sweet flavor. We
walked through a petting zoo, and I ran my fingers through
the soft fur of a goat. At night, the fireworks show started.
I heard a crackling sound and then a loud boom. I watched as
the dark sky exploded with beautiful colors. What a great day!

Smell: I could smell hot dogs and hamburgers cooking and sizzling on the grill.

Taste: _____

_____

Touch: _____

_____

Sound: _____

_____

Sight: _____

_____

Now think about a place you visited recently. Write your
own narrative using sensory details.

I went to _____.

I saw _____.

It smelled like _____.

I touched a _____ and it felt _____

_____.

I heard _____.

I ate a _____ and it tasted like _____

_____.

Times by 12

Multiply. Then write the correct answers in the boxes.

12 × ☐ = 144
W

12 × ☐ = 108
L

☐ × 12 = 36
A

12 × 5 = ☐
O

12 × 3 = ☐
H

☐ × 12 = 132
S

12 × ☐ = 12
C

12 × 2 = ☐
E

10 × 12 = ☐
T

☐ × 12 = 72
F

8 × 12 = ☐
N

12 × 6 = ☐
I

12 × ☐ = 0
I

☐ × 12 = 84
T

12 × ☐ = 120
O

☐ × 12 = 96
S

12 × ☐ = 24
E

7 × 12 = ☐
V

12 × 12 = ☐
E

To solve the riddle, write the letter that goes with each answer on the line.

Riddle: Why is the longest human nose only 11 inches long?

Answer: Because ____ ____ ____ ____ ____ ____
           120   12   2   9   84   24

____ ____ ____ ____ ____ ____   ____ ____   ____
 0   96   1   36   144   11   72   8   3

____ ____ ____ ____
 6   10   60   7

What's Happening?

Read each story about a hobby. What hobby
is being described? Write your answer on the line.

1. Jada sat outside with her canvas. She looked at the flowers covered with dew. Then she used a brush to mix the colors exactly right. Jada always had an eye for beauty.

   _____

2. Ming felt the warm soil in her hands. It was perfect! Springtime had just begun, and the earth was ready. Ming gently dropped seeds into small holes in the soil.

   _____

3. Sari balanced on her board as salty water splashed her face. She rode the wave all the way to the shore. She needed more sunscreen before she went out again.

   _____

4. Robby added two eggs to the batter. He used the mixer to make sure all the ingredients were combined. After he put the batter in the oven, the smell of chocolate cake filled the house.

   _____

5. Wan stood at the top of the hill. A blanket of sparkling white snow lay before him. As he took off, the cold wind nipped at his nose and his ears. Powder flew up around his board.

   _____

6. Kate sat quietly under the tree with her notebook. Line for line, she wrote a verse about her favorite season—fall. She paused to think of words that rhyme with *wind*.

   _____

Capital Carnival

Find the words that need to be capitalized in
each sentence and write them on the lines.

1. I have two cousins, hans and brian. _____Hans_____ _____Brian_____

2. They live in atlanta, georgia. _____ _____

3. We always go visit them on christmas. _____

4. This year, we visited them on independence day, too. _____ _____

5. We all went to a carnival on the fourth of july. _____ _____

6. There was a giant cake that looked like an american flag. _____

7. I saw people dressed like soldiers from the revolutionary war. _____
   _____

8. During the fireworks show, they played "the star-spangled banner."
   _____ _____ _____ _____

9. I hear that the best fireworks show is in washington, d.c. _____
   _____

10. I want to visit my cousins again next july! _____

Maze of Millions

Find the maze path that has numbers ordered from smallest to largest.

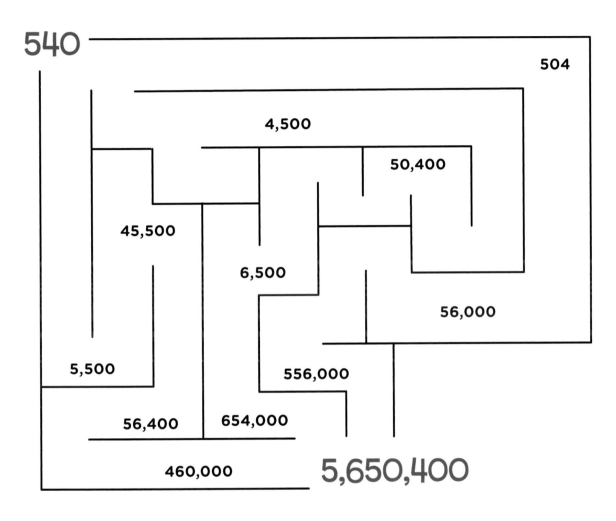

Now complete the chart below by rounding off each
number to the nearest thousand, ten thousand, and hundred thousand.

	THOUSAND	TEN THOUSAND	HUNDRED THOUSAND
385,990	386,000	390,000	400,000
712,183			
149,230			
534,769			

Page by Page

The students in Mrs. Gill's class are having a reading contest.
Each student has several more pages to read. Write the number
of the last page of the book on the line.

1. Dina has 10 more pages to read.

34 ____

2. Viet has 5 more pages to read.

42 ____

3. Raul has 13 more pages to read.

27 ____

4. Jen has 4 more pages to read.

31 ____

5. Kim has 18 more pages to read.

28 ____

6. Albert has 22 more pages to read.

19 ____

7. Sophie has 16 more pages to read.

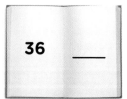

36 ____

8. Kenny has 25 more pages to read.

15 ____

If all the students finished their books…

9. Who read the most pages? _____

10. Who read the fewest pages? _____

11. How many pages did the students read altogether? _____

What It's All About

The **main idea** tells what a paragraph is mostly about.
Read each paragraph. Then circle the main idea.

1. The great pyramids were built in Egypt about 4,500 years ago. To this day, scientists still don't know how they were built. Scientists have lots of ideas but aren't sure how ancient people lifted and placed the stones so perfectly. Scientists think the Egyptians used the stars to guide them.

   The great pyramids are tombs.
   Egypt has many large pyramids.
   No one knows how the pyramids were built.

2. More than anything, Jeremy wanted to make the basketball team. Every day after school, he practiced in the gym. He had also been practicing jump shots in his backyard. He knew that the more he practiced, the better chance he had at getting on the team.

   Jeremy loves basketball.
   Jeremy wants to make the basketball team.
   Jeremy plays basketball in his backyard.

3. Spiders are not insects; they are called arachnids. Unlike insects, arachnids have eight legs rather than six. They also have two body parts rather than three. Spiders spin webs to catch food. Insects don't spin webs because they don't have spinnerets, as spiders do.

   Spiders are arachnids.
   Spiders are different from insects.
   Insects can't spin webs.

4. Television is not good for your health. How can television be unhealthful? It keeps people from getting the exercise they need! Instead of plopping down in front of the television today, go outside and play a game or go to the park. Try not to watch television for a week, and see what other activities you can come up with!

   Watching television can be unhealthful.
   Television is bad for society.
   People who don't watch television exercise more.

Pattern Party

Fill in the blanks to continue each pattern.

1. ■ ▲ ◆ ● ■ △ ◆ ○ ____ ____

2. ● ● ▲ ● ● ▲ ____ ____ ____

3. ■ ■ ◆ ▲ ____ ____ ____ ____

4. 5   10 ____ 20 ____ ____ 35 ____

5. 4   6   8 ____ 12   14 ____ 18

6. a   a   b   c   a   a ____ ____ a ____ b ____

Figure the Fractions

Look at each set of objects. What fraction of the set is circled?

1.

  a) $\dfrac{2}{3}$ b) $\dfrac{4}{8}$

  c) $\dfrac{6}{12}$ d) $\dfrac{1}{4}$

2.

  a) $\dfrac{5}{5}$ b) $\dfrac{1}{5}$

  c) $\dfrac{2}{5}$ d) $\dfrac{2}{6}$

3.

  a) $\dfrac{1}{3}$ b) $\dfrac{3}{6}$

  c) $\dfrac{4}{9}$ d) $\dfrac{6}{9}$

4.

  a) $\dfrac{5}{12}$ b) $\dfrac{1}{2}$

  c) $\dfrac{3}{4}$ d) $\dfrac{8}{12}$

5.

  a) $\dfrac{2}{3}$ b) $\dfrac{2}{4}$

  c) $\dfrac{1}{3}$ d) $\dfrac{2}{6}$

6. Color the fraction shown.

  a) $\dfrac{1}{3}$

  b) $\dfrac{4}{7}$

7.

  a) $\dfrac{1}{2}$ b) $\dfrac{4}{10}$

  c) $\dfrac{2}{3}$ d) $\dfrac{5}{10}$

Fact or Opinion?

A **fact** is true and can be proven. An **opinion** is how you feel about something. Write **F** for **fact** and **O** for **opinion** for each statement below.

> **Fact:** August 29 is my birthday.
>
> **Opinion:** I love birthday parties.

1. Mt. Everest is the tallest mountain in the world. _____

2. I think it would be exciting to climb Mt. Everest. _____

3. The first American reached the summit in 1963. _____

4. Mt. Everest is on the border between Nepal and Tibet. _____

5. It's scary knowing some people have never returned. _____

6. Each year, it seems more people want to climb it. _____

7. Sherman Bull, 64, is the oldest person to reach the summit. _____

8. Mt. Everest must be the coldest place on Earth. _____

9. From the summit, one must feel like a hero! _____

10. Winds at the peak blow at more than 118 miles per hour. _____

Write a fact and an opinion about a place you have visited.

Fact: _____

Opinion: _____

Animal Appetites

This food web shows us what animals eat.

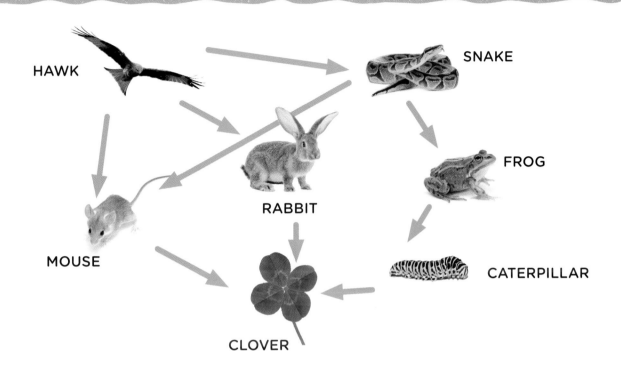

HAWK

SNAKE

FROG

RABBIT

MOUSE

CATERPILLAR

CLOVER

An **herbivore** is an animal that eats plants. Which animals in the web are herbivores?

1. _____

_____

_____

A **carnivore** is an animal that eats meat. Which animals in the web are carnivores?

2. _____

_____

_____

A **predator** is an animal that stalks and eats other animals.
A predator's victim is called **prey**. Use the food web to complete the chart.

Predator	Prey
frog	
snake	_____ , _____
	rabbit
_____ , _____	mouse

Word Play

Complete the activity below.

Find the meaning for the bold word in each sentence.

1. Doug swung at the ball with a **bat**.

    a) a long, wooden club

    b) a small, black animal with wings

2. The other team dropped the ball and it started to **roll** away.

    a) a small round piece of bread

    b) to turn over and over

3. The crowd **rose** to its feet and cheered.

    a) to become higher

    b) a flower

4. Doug set a school **record** for the most home runs.

    a) a thin, black disc for playing music

    b) the best performance

Find the sentence with the same meaning for the bold word.

5. Doug's team was so happy they **beat** the other team.

    a) The chef beat the eggs with a whisk.

    b) My brother can never beat me at checkers.

6. Doug even had a **tear** in his eye!

    a) A big tear rolled down the baby's cheek.

    b) You should never tear a page out of a book.

Write It Out

Complete the activity below.

Write out each number in thousands, hundreds, tens, and ones.

1. 5,337

_____ = _____ + _____ + _____ + _____

2. 1,095

_____ = _____ + _____ + _____ + _____

3. 4,198

_____ = _____ + _____ + _____ + _____

4. 6,441

_____ = _____ + _____ + _____ + _____

5. 7,720

_____ = _____ + _____ + _____ + _____

6. Write as many 3-digit numbers as you can using: 6, 3, 8.

_____

_____

_____

Now circle the smallest number. Then cross out the largest number.

Making New Words with Prefixes

A **prefix** is a word part added to the front of a base word to make a new word. A prefix changes the meaning of that word.

Read the meanings of the prefixes in the box.

re- again	**non-** no, not
pre- before	**un-** not
mis- wrong	**tri-** three

Add the prefix to each word to make a new word. Then draw a line to the definition for the new word.

1. mis + direct _____   not load

2. pre + date _____   date before

3. re + appear _____   shape with three angles

4. tri + cycle _____   not for profit

5. non + profit _____   direct wrongly

6. mis + spell _____   not cover

7. pre + heat _____   appear again

8. un + load _____   no sense

9. non + sense _____   cycle with three wheels

10. re + read _____   heat before

11. tri + angle _____   spell wrong

12. un + cover _____   read again

Combination Vacation

Read each pair of sentences. Combine the sentences by using commas, adding small words, or leaving words out. Rewrite the new sentence on the line.

1. I went on vacation with my mom and dad. My sister Amy went with us.

_____

2. We drove south on the California coast and stopped in three cities. We stopped in San Francisco, Santa Barbara, and San Diego.

_____

_____

3. It was a long drive, so I read a book. I also listened to the radio.

_____

4. In San Francisco we saw the Golden Gate Bridge. We went to a museum, too.

_____

5. I swam in the ocean in Santa Barbara. Amy and Mom swam with me.

_____

6. San Diego was my favorite place. I liked the zoo.

_____

7. We saw monkeys and gorillas. We saw apes, too.

_____

8. Amy liked the tigers the best. I thought they were too scary.

_____

Food Factors

Factors are numbers that you can multiply to equal a product. Factors are always in pairs.

If you have 12 jelly beans you can group them in three different ways.

$1 \times 12 = 12$ $\qquad\qquad$ $12 \times 1 = 12$

$2 \times 6 = 12$ $\qquad$ $6 \times 2 = 12$ $\qquad\qquad$ $3 \times 4 = 12$ $\qquad$ $4 \times 3 = 12$

The factors of 12 are
1, 2, 3, 4, 6, 12.

You have 6 apples total. How many equal groups can you make?

___ × ___ = 6 $\qquad$ ___ × ___ = 6

___ × ___ = 6

___ × ___ = 6

The factors of 6 are

___ , ___ , ___ , ___ .

Making New Words with Suffixes

A suffix is a word part added to the end of a base word to make a
new word. A suffix changes the meaning of that word.
Read the meanings of the suffixes in the box.

-ful	full of
-ly	like, resembling
-ness	state or quality of
-less	without
-er/or	one who
-able	is, can be

Read the definitions below. Make a new word to
match each definition by adding a suffix.

1. someone who acts   _____

2. a happy state   _____

3. without joy   _____

4. like a prince   _____

5. someone who teaches   _____

6. full of care   _____

7. can have comfort   _____

8. state of being kind   _____

Add **-ful**, **-ly**, **-less**, **-er**, **-or**, or **-able** to each word in **( )** that best completes
the sentence. Write the new word on the line.

9. James is studying to be a (paint) at the School for Fine Arts. _____

10. Min is (care) when she spends money without thinking. _____

11. Nick (selfish) took all the cookies for himself. _____

12. Everyone loves Keri's happy nature and (cheer) smile. _____

Prime Time!

There are 13 prime numbers between 1 and 50. Can you find all
13 inside the TV set? Circle all the prime numbers!

$1 \times 3 = 3$ $3 \times 1 = 1$

The number 3 has only two factors,
so it's a prime number.

A **prime number** is a number
that has exactly two factors.
The factors are 1 and itself.

Tracking Time

Draw hands on the clocks to show the times.

1. 1 hour past 4:30

2. 2 hours before 11:00

3. 45 minutes after 7:15

4. 3 hours before 3:20

5. 2 hours after 2:10

6. 1 hour and 15 minutes after 9:00

7. $1\frac{1}{2}$ hours before 7:30

8. 3 hours and 15 minutes after 11:15

9. What time do you wake up?

10. What time do you start school?

11. What time do you eat dinner?

12. What time do you go to bed?

Preposition Puzzle

Prepositions link and relate a noun or a pronoun to another word in a sentence. Common prepositions include **in**, **on**, **up**, **for**, **at**, **of**, **with**, **to**, **before**, and **after**. Underline the preposition in each sentence. Then circle it in the word search. Words can go across, down, or diagonal.

1. The kitten is running around the basket.
2. The monkey is screeching for a banana.
3. Several eagles soared over the canyon.
4. Our dog loves hiding underneath the bed.
5. A tiny mouse stored crumbs inside the box.
6. We could hear the wolves howling before sunset.
7. The panther slunk quietly through the rainforest.
8. Snakes usually sleep during the day when it's hot.
9. Dolphins swam with the boat all afternoon.
10. A beautiful chestnut horse ran across the beach.

J	A	D	O	U	T	D	C	E	O	H
A	R	O	U	N	D	Y	B	A	T	S
Z	F	T	O	R	R	M	E	A	H	T
W	O	N	A	E	I	R	E	G	R	A
A	R	I	V	C	E	N	B	V	O	W
M	P	O	D	A	R	I	G	R	U	P
C	W	U	B	E	F	O	R	E	G	E
E	T	I	D	R	V	A	S	H	H	U
R	S	N	T	M	E	T	W	S	I	P
F	U	P	R	H	I	N	T	L	D	E
J	T	E	I	N	S	I	D	E	G	A

Ecosystems Are Everywhere

Read the passage and complete the activity below.

What do a small sand dune and a huge desert have in common? Both are ecosystems! An ecosystem is any community of plants and animals and the environment they live in. All of the living things in an ecosystem interact with each other. Here are a few common types of ecosystems:

Coastal: Beaches, oceans, marine areas

Forest: Tree-filled woodlands

ECOSYSTEM

Freshwater: Rivers, streams, and lakes

Urban: Cities and towns filled with people

Grassland: Grassy meadows and prairies where cattle graze

Write the name of the ecosystem that best describes each place.

1. Tide pools _____ coastal _____

2. New York City _____

3. A mountainside of pine trees _____

4. Lake Michigan _____

5. A cow pasture _____

6. A coral reef _____

7. A busy street with skyscrapers _____

8. The Mississippi River _____

No Ordinary Order

Read the story. Then number the sentences **1** to **8**
to show the correct order of events.

Stacy and Sarah spent all morning rollerblading at the park. Soon, it was lunchtime and the girls were hungry.

"Let's go get a hamburger at the Burger Barn," Stacy suggested.

"That sounds good," said Sarah, "but the Burger Barn is too far to walk."

"It's not too far to rollerblade there," said Stacy.

"Good idea. Let's go!" Sarah said.

The girls rollerbladed to Burger Barn. When they got there, they went to the window and ordered burgers, fries, and soda.

"Let's rollerblade while we wait for our food," said Stacy.

Sarah said, "Okay! It will be fun. I'll race you!"

The girls took off toward the park.

Suddenly, Stacy stopped. "Oh, no," she said. "We forgot to pick up our food! We were so excited about racing to the park, we left our food at the window!"

_____ Stacy suggested that the girls rollerblade while they wait for their food.

_____ The girls took off toward the park.

_____ It was lunchtime and the girls were getting hungry.

_____ They decided to rollerblade to the Burger Barn.

_____ Sarah suggested that the girls race.

_____ Stacy and Sarah rollerbladed around the park.

_____ They realized that they had left their food at the Burger Barn!

_____ Stacy and Sarah ordered their food.

Understanding Poetry

Read the poem "The Wind" by Robert Louis Stevenson.
Then answer the questions.

I saw you toss the kites on high
And blow the birds about the sky;
And all around I heard you pass,
Like ladies' skirts across the grass—
    O wind, a-blowing all day long,
    O wind, that sings so loud a song!

I saw the different things you did,
But always you yourself you hid.
I felt you push, I heard you call,
I could not see yourself at all—
    O wind, a-blowing all day long,
    O wind, that sings so loud a song!

O you that are so strong and cold,
O blower, are you young or old?
Are you a beast of field and tree,
Or just a stronger child than me?
    O wind, a-blowing all day long,
    O wind, that sings so loud a song!

1. To whom is the speaker talking? _____

2. Who is the speaker in the poem? _____

3. Write the three rhyming word pairs from the first verse.

_____ _____ _____

_____ _____ _____

4. Write two lines that give the wind human traits. _____

_____

5. Which two rhyming words are repeated three times?

_____ _____

The Art of the Apostrophe

Complete the activity below.

A **contraction** is two words put together to make one. For example, *he will* becomes *he'll*. A **possessive** shows that someone owns the thing that comes after the possessive. For example, *the flowers that belong to Mom* becomes *Mom's flowers*. An **apostrophe** tells whether a word is a contraction or a possessive. Use apostrophes to form new words below.

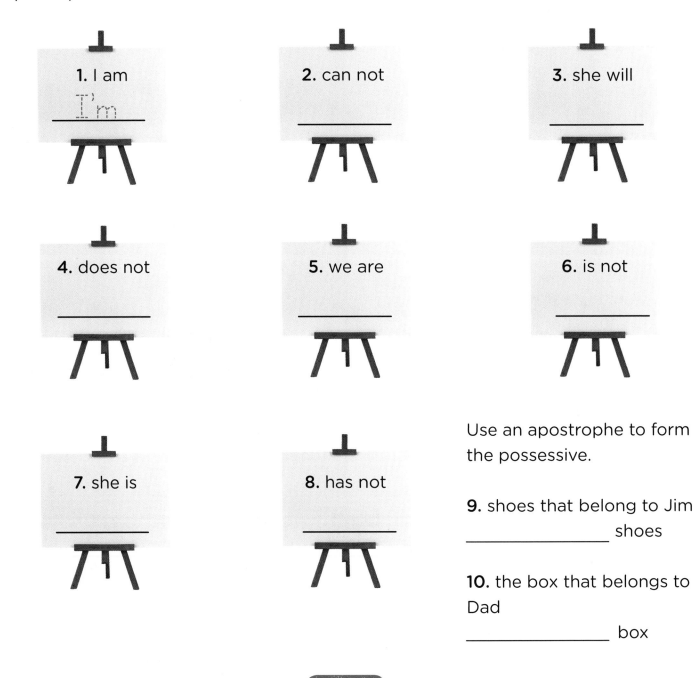

1. I am

I'm

2. can not

_____

3. she will

_____

4. does not

_____

5. we are

_____

6. is not

_____

7. she is

_____

8. has not

_____

Use an apostrophe to form the possessive.

9. shoes that belong to Jim

_____ shoes

10. the box that belongs to Dad

_____ box

Get into Shape

Complete the activity below.

The **perimeter** of a shape is the total distance around its sides. To get the perimeter, add all the sides together. The **area** is the amount of space taken up by the entire shape. To get the area, multiply the length by the width. Always write the area with the unit of measurement and the squared sign.

20 yards

10 yards

Perimeter = 20 + 20 + 10 + 10 = 60 yards.

Area = 20 × 10 = 200 yards²

Find the perimeter and the area of each shape.

1. 5 cm

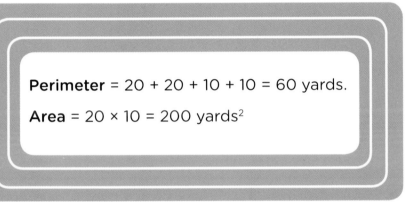

Perimeter = ___ + ___ + ___ + ___ = ___ cm
Area = ___ × ___ = ___ cm²

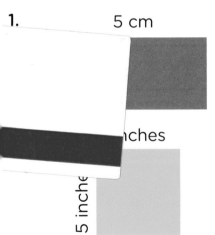

5 inches   nches

Perimeter = ___ + ___ + ___ + ___ = ___ in
Area = ___ × ___ = ___ in²

4 cm

3. 7 ft

2 ft

Perimeter = _____
Area = _____

4 cm

Perimeter = _____
Area = _____

8 in

1 in

Perimeter = _____
Area = _____

Mountain Time

Read this bus schedule for the campsites at Bear Mountain.
Then answer the questions.

Bus	To	Departs	Arrives
3	Deer Valley	8:15 AM	10:00 AM
5	Great Gorge	9:05 AM	12:10 PM
7	Rattlesnake River	11:30 AM	1:30 PM
9	Moon Meadow	1:45 PM	5:30 PM
11	Ragged Rock	3:20 PM	5:40 PM
13	Shadow Lake	4:00 PM	7:30 PM

1. Which bus has the shortest trip? _____

2. Which bus has the longest trip? _____

3. How long is the trip to Rattlesnake River? _____

4. How long is the trip to Ragged Rock? _____

5. How much longer is the trip to Moon Meadow than to Shadow Lake?

_____

6. How much longer is the trip to Ragged Rock than to Deer Valley?

_____

7. The bus to Great Gorge is 2 hours late. What time will it arrive?

_____

8. The bus to Deer Valley is 1 hour, 15 minutes late. What time will it arrive?

_____

Writing a Friendly Letter

Complete the activity below.

33 J Street
Snowy, MN 22591
July 16, 2006

Heading: The heading is your address and the date. Or it can just be the date.

Greeting: This is the opening of the letter. It usually starts with the word **Dear** and ends with a comma.

Dear Manny,

    I went to surf with my brother yesterday. He taught me how to stand on the board. I rode a few waves. I even did it without falling down! It was really fun! I think I'm going to take lessons. Then maybe my parents will buy me my own surfboard.

    I hope you are having a great summer. Write me a letter and tell me what you've been doing.

Body: This is the main part of the letter. Indent each new paragraph.

Your friend,

Josie

Signature: This is where you sign your name.

Closing: This is where the letter ends. It says good-bye with words like **Your friend**, **From**, or **Love**. The first letter in the closing is capitalized and then it ends with a comma.

On another sheet of paper, write a letter to a friend or a family member. Tell this person about a new activity you've tried or a place you've visited. Remember to follow these rules:

- Use interesting words.
- Use correct punctuation.
- Use complete sentences.

Math Magic

Complete the division and multiplication problems.

1. 2435
   × 71
   _____

2. 7645
   × 56
   _____

3. 9310
   × 13
   _____

4. 7628
   × 29
   _____

5. 9025
   × 52
   _____

6. 5471
   × 34
   _____

7. 3) 6750

8. 7) 6741

9. 5) 3490

10. 6) 2190

11. 9) 5868

12. 2) 1270

Vote for Me!

Read about how we elect our leaders. Then solve the riddles below!

President

There is only one president at a time. A president serves for four years. A president can be reelected only one time. So, the longest time a president can serve is for eight years total. You must be at least 35 years old to run for president.

Senator

Every state has two senators. Senators serve for six years. You must be at least 30 years old to run for senator.

Representative

The number of representatives is different for each state. The higher the population, the more representatives a state has. There are always 435 representatives total. You must be 25 years old to run. A representative serves for two years.

1. I serve for four years and can be reelected one time. What am I?

   president

2. There are two of me from every state. What am I?

   _____

3. Each state has a different number of me, depending on its population. California has 53 of me. Rhode Island has two. What am I?

   _____

4. There is only one of me at a time! I am at least 35 years old. What am I?

   _____

5. There are 435 of me total. I serve for two years. What am I?

   _____

6. I serve for six years. I am always at least 30 years old. What am I?

   _____

Magic Squares

All rows and columns in these "magic" squares add up to the magic number. Can you complete the magic squares? Hint: You can only use each number once in each magic square.

1. All rows and columns add up to **12**.

7		3
0	4	
	6	

2. All rows and columns add up to **21**.

6		5
	3	
	8	

3. All rows and columns add up to **15**.

2		
7	5	
		8

4. All rows and columns add up to **25**.

	5	7
3		
		12

5. All rows and columns add up to **18**.

	1	
7		5
	11	

6. All rows and columns add up to **30**.

12		1
	13	
11		

Convince Me

Complete the activity below.

A **persuasive paragraph** tries to convince someone of something. The writer gives pros and cons of the subject and tries to get readers to agree with his or her point of view. The writer must use reasons to support his or her opinion.

Choose one of these topics:
- Should students choose the lunch menu in the cafeteria?
- Should schools extend summer vacation by one month?
- Should you have a later bedtime?

List some reasons why this is a good idea (pros) or bad idea (cons).

Pros	Cons

What do you think? Choose one side of your topic to argue. On another sheet of paper, write a paragraph trying to convince your parents to agree with your opinion. Give at least three reasons to support it.

Pollen Power

Read the passage and complete the activity below.

Female plants need to make new seeds, but they can't do it on their own. They need to get a special yellow dust, called pollen, from male plants. This is called pollination. The pollen travels from one plant to the next.

Sometimes the wind carries the pollen from one plant to another. Sometimes different insects, such as bees, can carry the pollen. As bees land on flowers to drink their nectar, some of the pollen gets stuck to them. When they fly to the next flower, the pollen falls off. Larger animals, such as hummingbirds, do the same thing. Pollen can also be carried by water.

Pollination can happen a few different ways. What's important is that the pollen gets to the female plant so that new seeds can be made!

1. Name four ways that pollen travels:

_____ wind _____   _____

_____   _____

2. Number the sentences **1** through **5** to show the correct order of events.

_____ Some pollen lands on a female plant.

_____ A big gust of wind comes along and carries the pollen with it.

_____ The plant is pollinated, and a new seed is made.

_____ A male plant has a yellow dust called pollen.

_____ The seed is planted and a new plant begins to grow.

Double Bubble

Read both passages. Answer the questions to complete the chart below. Compare the answers for each paragraph.

A.

Modern-day chewing gum was actually invented by accident! A man from Mexico was looking for a substitute for rubber. He asked an inventor named Thomas Adams to experiment with a substance called chicle. The chicle didn't work as a rubber substitute. However, as Adams discovered, it did make a tasty chewing gum!

B.

Betty wanted to make the biggest bubble ever. She put lots of gumballs in her mouth and chewed them. Then, she blew a giant bubble. Just as she was admiring her bubble, a big gust of wind came along. The bubble popped all over her face!

	Passage A	Passage B
1. Is the passage fiction or nonfiction?	nonfiction	
2. What is the main idea of the passage?		
3. What is a good title for the passage?		

Counting Shapes

Count the shapes below. Hint: Two or more small shapes can be inside bigger shapes.

1. How many triangles are in this shape? _____

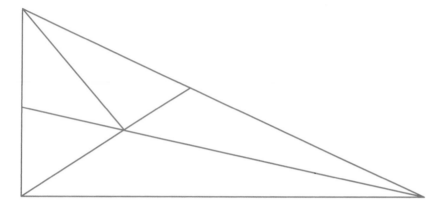

2. How many squares are in this shape? _____

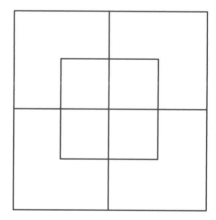

3. How many rectangles are in this shape? _____

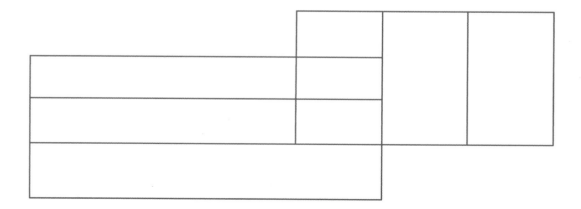

Same Spelling, Different Meanings

Some words have several meanings.

> **Example:**
> Lauren finally got her turn at <u>bat</u>.
> A big, black <u>bat</u> flew right over my head!

Read each set of sentences. Look at the underlined words. Then circle the letter for the sentence that matches the meaning in the first sentence.

1. A large brown <u>bear</u> walked through our camp.
   a) Can you <u>bear</u> the weight of those boxes?
   b) The <u>bear</u> played with its cubs in the meadow.

2. Several kittens are hidden inside the <u>brush</u>.
   a) Trim the <u>brush</u> back below the windows.
   b) <u>Brush</u> your teeth before you go to bed.

3. Put your coats <u>down</u> on the bed.
   a) The canoe is all the way <u>down</u> the river.
   b) Each fluffy pillow was filled with <u>down</u>.

4. <u>Pound</u> the dough until it is flat.
   a) The little puppy barely weighs a <u>pound</u>.
   b) Jack can <u>pound</u> the ball right over the fence.

5. Sara <u>felt</u> sad when summer vacation ended.
   a) Tham cut different shapes from purple and red <u>felt</u>.
   b) Most of the team <u>felt</u> the umpire made some bad calls.

6. A mother <u>duck</u> led her ducklings across the road.
   a) <u>Duck</u> your head if you don't want to get wet!
   b) A male <u>duck</u> is called a drake.

7. The <u>ground</u> shook violently during the earthquake.
   a) Red and yellow leaves are all over the <u>ground</u>.
   b) Keisha <u>ground</u> the nuts into a fine powder.

8. Sometimes students can be <u>mean</u> to one another.
   a) Lisa didn't <u>mean</u> to hurt your feelings.
   b) The <u>mean</u>, angry lion wouldn't share its food.

Now, write a story using all the underlined words: **bear, brush, down, pound, felt, duck, ground,** and **mean**. Use the meanings you circled and your imagination!

_____

_____

_____

_____

Funny Fractions

If a numerator and denominator in a fraction are the same number, the fraction is equal to 1. If a fraction below is equal to 1, circle the letter. Write all the circled letters in order on the lines below to answer the riddle.

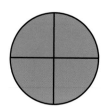

$$\frac{4}{4} = 1$$

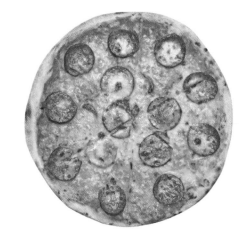

A
$$\frac{4}{4}$$

T
$$\frac{1}{2}$$

P
$$\frac{2}{2}$$

O
$$\frac{3}{2}$$

I
$$\frac{9}{9}$$

E
$$\frac{5}{5}$$

I
$$\frac{11}{11}$$

N
$$\frac{3}{3}$$

O
$$\frac{2}{22}$$

T
$$\frac{6}{6}$$

H
$$\frac{10}{10}$$

E
$$\frac{8}{8}$$

I
$$\frac{6}{9}$$

T
$$\frac{11}{1}$$

S
$$\frac{7}{7}$$

K
$$\frac{1}{1}$$

Y
$$\frac{12}{12}$$

E
$$\frac{7}{1}$$

What do you call a flying pizza?

A __ __ __ __   __ __ __ __   __ __ __

Easy Money

Look at the code below. Each letter of the alphabet is worth the dollar amount shown. Use these amounts to make the "money words" below.

A = $1
B = $2
C = $3
D = $4
E = $5
F = $6
G = $7
H = $8
I = $9

J = $10
K = $11
L = $12
M = $13
N = $14
O = $15
P = $16
Q = $17
R = $18

S = $19
T = $20
U = $21
V = $22
W = $23
X = $24
Y = $25
Z = $26

EXAMPLE: ADDITION
$1 + $4 + $4 + $9 + $20 + $9 + $15 + $14 = $76 word

1. What is your first name worth?

_____

2. What is your last name worth?

_____

3. What is the name of your school worth?

_____

4. What is the name of your favorite sport worth?

_____

5. What is the name of your favorite food worth?

_____

6. Write a word that is worth exactly $10.

_____

7. Write a word that is worth between $40 and $50.

_____

8. Write a word that is worth more than $100.

_____

9. Write the most expensive word you can.

_____

10. Write the least expensive word you can.

_____

A Surprise Helper

Read the story. Then answer the questions below.

Katie had been in a wheelchair for almost a year. After the accident, her legs did not work the way they should. Katie had been working hard to get better, but she knew it would be a long time before she could walk again. In the meantime, she needed help around the house. She had trouble getting her wheelchair in places where she could turn lights on and off, brush her teeth, or even answer the door. Her parents couldn't be with her 24 hours a day. So they decided to get her a helper.

Katie couldn't believe it when her parents came home with a capuchin monkey named Binx. "What can a monkey do to help me?" Katie sighed. Mom smiled. "Just watch! Lights, Binx!" Binx jumped over to the light switch and flipped it off. "Brush, Binx," Mom said. Binx grabbed Katie's hairbrush and started brushing her hair. Katie couldn't keep from giggling.

"He can do almost anything," Dad said. "He can pull out chairs, push elevator buttons, carry your backpack, and use the TV and DVD player. His hands are so much like human hands, he can get you almost anything you need."

Katie grinned and pointed to a soda on the counter. "Get soda," she said. Binx grabbed the can and gave it to Katie. Then he sat on her lap and put his head on her shoulder. "You guys are the best," Katie said, smiling.

1. Who is the main character in this story? _____

2. Where does the story take place? _____

3. What problem does Katie have at the beginning of the story? _____
_____
_____

4. How is the problem solved? _____
_____

5. What do you think will happen next in the story? _____
_____
_____

Fraction Fun

Complete the activity below.

A **mixed number** is a whole number and a fraction. For example, $1\frac{1}{3}$ is a mixed number. You can change an improper fraction to a mixed number with a proper fraction. Change each improper fraction below into a mixed number with a proper fraction.

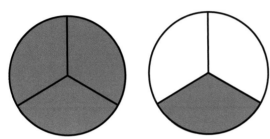

$$\frac{4}{3} = \frac{3}{3} + \frac{1}{3} = 1\frac{1}{3}$$

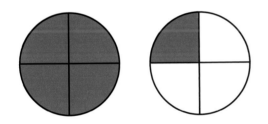

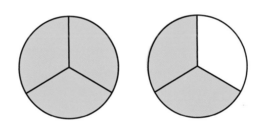

1. $\dfrac{5}{4} = \dfrac{4}{4} + \dfrac{1}{4} = $ _____

2. $\dfrac{5}{3} = \dfrac{3}{3} + \dfrac{2}{3} = $ _____

3. $\dfrac{7}{5} = \dfrac{5}{5} + \dfrac{2}{5} = $ _____

4. $\dfrac{8}{6} = \dfrac{6}{6} + \dfrac{2}{6} = $ _____

5. $\dfrac{5}{3} = \dfrac{3}{3} + $ _____ $= $ _____

6. $\dfrac{3}{2} = \dfrac{2}{2} + $ _____ $= $ _____

7. $\dfrac{6}{5} = $ _____ $+ $ _____ $= $ _____

8. $\dfrac{8}{5} = $ _____ $+ $ _____ $= $ _____

Governor Word Guess

Learn about the job of a governor as you read the passage.
Fill in each blank with a word from the word list.

mansion
educational
budget
vote
taxes
governor
fifty
constitution
laws
citizens

The United States of America is made up of (1) ___fifty___ different states,

and each one is unique! Each state has its own government and even its own

(2) _____. The leader of a state is called a (3) _____.

A governor is elected by the (4) _____ of the state. So, if you live

in New Jersey, you can't (5) _____ for the governor of Colorado.

The governor has a very busy job. A governor helps handle the state's money

and oversees the (6) _____. He or she has to make sure that the

state collects (7) _____. He or she also has to watch over the

(8) _____ system and make sure the schools are doing a good job.

The governor helps make and pass (9) _____ for the state. This is

a tough job and a lot of work, but there is one perk. The governor gets to live in

the governor's (10) _____ while he's in office!

Across the Ages

Read each problem carefully. Then solve it.

There are five people in the Tanaka family. Their ages are 41, 45, 13, 17, and 9.

1. What is the difference between the oldest and the youngest member of the family? _____

2. What is the average age of all the family members?
_____

3. What fraction of the family members are younger than 40? _____

4. Suni is 8 years younger than the mean age. How old is Suni? _____

The total of Mario's, Ana's, and Jose's ages is 25. Jose is 36 months old.

5. Ana is three times older than Jose. How old is she? _____

6. How old is Mario? _____

7. In 10 years, how old will the children be?

Mario: _____

Ana: _____

Jose: _____

Five cousins are the following ages: Jill is 16 $\frac{1}{2}$, Tom is 13, Jared is 15 $\frac{1}{2}$, Penny is 16, and Sara is 14.

8. What is the total of all of their ages? _____

9. What is the average age of all the cousins? _____

10. What is the difference in age between the oldest and the youngest cousin?
_____

11. Which cousin will be 25 in 9 $\frac{1}{2}$ years? _____

Staci is 12 years older than Mike. Mike is twice as old as Darryl. Shana is 7 years younger than Chris. Chris is 15 years older than Darryl. Mike is 12.

12. How old is Staci? _____

13. How old is Darryl? _____

14. How old is Shana? _____

15. How old is Chris? _____

In the Almanac

An **almanac** contains thousands of facts and figures on almost any topic you can think of. A **table of contents** shows the major sections in a book. It is in the front of a book, before the body. You can use it to help find major topics or chapters.

Use this table of contents in the almanac to answer the questions.

Contents

1. On what page does Famous Scientists begin? _____

2. On what page does U.S. State Products end? _____

3. You want to find the height of Mt. Whitney. In what section would you look?
_____

4. You want to find out who won the 1908 presidential election. In what section would you look? _____

5. You want to find out how many students go to Boston College. In what section would you look? _____

6. You want to find out about whale migration. In what section would you look?
_____

7. You want to find the zip code for Phoenix, Arizona. In what section would you look? _____

8. You are reading page 102. What section are you reading? _____
_____

Rock Search

Read about the three different types of rock. Then find each bold word in the word search below.

Igneous Rock
Igneous means made by heat, so it's no wonder that these rocks come from **volcanoes**! Melted rock, called **magma**, pushes through cracks in the Earth's crust. The lava cools and hardens into igneous rock.

Metamorphic Rock
Metamorphic rock is a rock that has changed. **Heat** and **pressure** change igneous and sedimentary rocks into metamorphic rock. In fact, the word *metamorphic* means "to **change**."

Sedimentary Rock
Sedimentary rocks are made of many **layers**. Layers of soil, sand, mud, and even seashells squeeze together and harden into rock. We can find **fossils** like dinosaur **bones** buried in sedimentary rock.

```
S  E  D  I  M  E  N  T  A  R  Y
E  V  M  A  E  C  H  P  R  G  E
D  F  A  M  T  A  M  O  R  L  Y
V  O  L  C  A  N  O  E  S  A  B
I  S  A  O  M  A  G  M  A  Y  O
G  S  Y  B  O  N  P  R  E  S  N
F  I  E  P  R  E  S  S  U  R  E
O  L  R  R  P  I  G  N  E  U  S
L  S  S  C  H  E  A  T  L  D  E
I  F  O  C  I  G  N  E  O  U  S
S  E  D  I  C  H  A  N  G  E  I
```

Pool Poetry

Complete the activity below.

A **simile** is a comparison using the words *like* or *as*.
The pool was as big as a lake!

A **metaphor** is when you say that one thing is another thing.
I was a long raft, floating and drifting on the water.

Personification is when you describe objects with human-like feelings or actions.
The hot sun nagged at me to go to the pool.

Read each sentence and decide if it uses a simile, metaphor, or personification. Check the correct column.

	Simile	Metaphor	Personification
1. It was so hot outside, it felt like an oven.	✓		
2. The cool water called out to me.			
3. I shot toward the water like a cannonball.			
4. The splash I made was as big as a tidal wave.			
5. The water felt like cold ice.			
6. I was a fish, darting through the water.			
7. The water danced around me and tickled my toes.			
8. The divers were graceful swans gliding through the air.			

Now write a few of your own!

Simile:_____

Metaphor:_____

Personification:_____

Number Challenge

Look at each set of numbers. Fill in the circle next to the correct answer.

1. Which statement is true?
- ○ 45.01 < 4.5
- ○ 450. < 45.01
- ○ .450 > 4.50
- ○ 450 > .045

2. Which statement is true?
- ○ .008 < .080
- ○ 8.0 > 80.0
- ○ .800 > 8.00
- ○ 800. < 0.80

3. Which set of numbers is listed from least to greatest?
- ○ 10.034 12,250 12,100 11,799
- ○ 87,100 86,200 85,300 84,400
- ○ 52,550 52,700 52,990 53,100
- ○ 75,330 75,400 74,950 74,748

4. Which set of numbers is listed from greatest to least?
- ○ 68,190 68,760 68,833 68,255
- ○ 93,650 93,500 93,245 93,115
- ○ 22,395 24,430 25,800 26,710
- ○ 45,333 44,200 44,280 45,275

5. Which number is written as 600,000 + 70,000 + 5,000 + 0 + 80 + 5?
- ○ 765,805
- ○ 675,580
- ○ 675,085
- ○ 670,585

6. Which number is written as 800,000 + 10,000 + 9,000 + 900 + 30 + 7?
- ○ 819,937
- ○ 891,973
- ○ 819,397
- ○ 891,973

7. Write these numbers in order, from least to greatest: 9.540, .9540, 95.40, .0954

_____

_____

_____

8. Write these numbers in order, from greatest to least: .0015, 1.50, .015, 15.00

_____

_____

_____

Vacation Clues

Use the clues to find the answers. Write your answers in the puzzle.

Isel is ready to go to Hawaii! First, though, she has to pack her **1**. Isel has never flown before, but she is excited about riding in an **2**. She has so many questions! How many **3** high will we be in the air? What does it feel like when we take off? Does the **4** still look blue when you're in it? Are the **5** like giant puffs of cotton? How long will it take us to get to Hawaii?

When Isel got to the **6**, she sat and watched planes take off. There were five of them lined up on the **7**. Each one left a curly trail of **8** behind it. "This is going to be the best **9** ever!" Isel told her mom. She couldn't wait to see the great island. All sides are surrounded by the Pacific **10**. "The **11** is warm and crystal clear," her mom said. "And the **12** is as white as sugar!"

Pick the Part

As you read the passage, figure out the part of speech for each bold word. Write the words in the correct column below.

During the middle of the nineteenth century, Americans **started** moving to the West. They hoped to settle down on new land, so they were called **settlers**. The **journey** west was very **challenging**. There weren't any cars, so people rode in covered wagons. **Big** groups of wagons **traveled** together in a wagon train.

The settlers **bravely** faced the 2,000-mile trip west. The wagons could not travel very **quickly**, so the **trip** took about six months. They crossed prairies, deserts, and steep mountains. They even had to ride across flooded rivers. There were so many wagons traveling at the same time, the trail **was** very **dusty**. The settlers **courageously** continued on until they reached the West.

Nouns	Verbs	Adjectives	Adverbs
_____	_____	_____	_____
_____	_____	_____	_____
_____	_____	_____	_____

How Much Does Joe Owe?

Complete the activity below.

Joe doesn't have enough money to buy what he wants. He has to borrow money. How much money does he owe? Use the number line to help. Write what Joe owes as a **negative number**, a number that is less than zero.

Joe has 4 dollars. He wanted to buy a hat for 6 dollars. How much does Joe owe?
Joe owes __2__ dollars.

__-2__

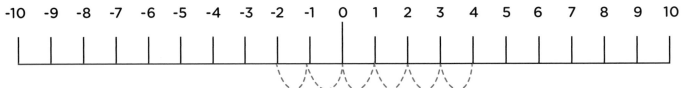

-10 -9 -8 -7 -6 -5 -4 -3 -2 -1   0   1   2   3   4   5   6   7   8   9   10

1. Joe had 2 dollars. He wanted to buy a burger for 4 dollars.
Joe owes _____ dollars.

_____

2. Joe had 3 dollars. He wanted to buy some shoes for 7 dollars.
Joe owes _____ dollars.

_____

3. Joe had 5 dollars. He wanted to buy a shirt for 8 dollars.
Joe owes _____ dollars.

_____

4. Joe had 2 dollars. He wanted to buy a game for 6 dollars.
Joe owes _____ dollars.

_____

5. Joe had 1 dollar. He wanted to buy a book for 3 dollars.
Joe owes _____ dollars.

_____

6. Joe had 4 dollars. He wanted to buy a pizza for 7 dollars.
Joe owes _____ dollars.

_____

Types of Writing

Complete the activity below.

There are many different styles of writing. Some of these include

Expository writing gives information and facts.
Narrative writing tells a story.
Descriptive writing "paints a picture" of a person, a place, or a thing.
Persuasive writing tries to convince someone of something.

Read each prompt below. Write the style of writing needed on each line:
expository, **narrative**, **descriptive**, or **persuasive**.

1. Think about a flower garden. What does it smell like? What kinds of colors do you see? Do you hear bees buzzing? On a separate piece of paper, write about the garden using your five senses. _____

2. On a separate piece of paper, explain how to build a model plane. Give step-by-step directions. _____

3. People drive way too fast down your street. You think the speed limit is too high. On a separate piece of paper, write an article convincing people to lower the speed limit.

   _____

4. Imagine that you just won the lottery! What would you do with the money? Who would you give it to? What would you buy? On a separate piece of paper, write a story about what you would do. _____

5. Fall is your favorite season. You love the smell of leaves burning. You love the taste of pumpkin pie. On a separate piece of paper, write about all the things you love about fall. _____

6. Do you remember your first day of school? Were you afraid? Did you like your first teacher? On a separate piece of paper, write a paragraph telling about everything that happened that day. _____

7. On a separate piece of paper, write an essay telling how to be safe in a thunderstorm. Include details listing things to do and not to do. _____

8. On a separate piece of paper, write a speech that convinces people why it is important to eat healthful foods and to exercise. _____

Lines, Shapes, and Angles

Geometry uses many special terms. Read each question. Pay close attention to any special terms. Then circle the correct answer.

1. Which shape has parallel lines?

a)   b)   c)

2. Which figure has a 90° angle?

a)   b)   c)

3. Which pair of lines is perpendicular?

a)   b)   c)

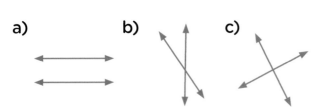

4. Which figure has a 180° angle?

a)   b)   c)

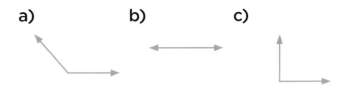

5. Which shape is an equilateral triangle?

a)   b)   c)

6. Which pair of shapes is congruent?

a)   b)   c)

7. Which shape has 4 angles?

a)   b)   c)

8. Which shape has a line of symmetry?

a)   b)   c)

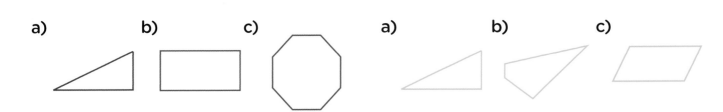

Rockin' Round Off

Complete the activity below.

A **whole number** is a number with no decimals. The numbers **1** and **2** are whole numbers. To round to the nearest whole number, look at the decimal. The number **1.7** would be rounded to **2**. Numbers exactly halfway, like 3.5, should be rounded up. Round each number to the nearest whole number.

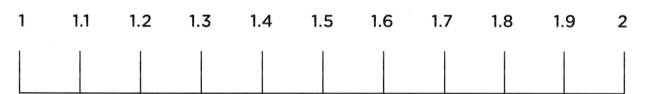

| 1 | 1.1 | 1.2 | 1.3 | 1.4 | 1.5 | 1.6 | 1.7 | 1.8 | 1.9 | 2 |

1. 1.2 _____   **2.** 1.9 _____

3. 2.4 _____   **4.** 3.6 _____

5. 4.1 _____   **6.** 5.8 _____

7. 3.3 _____   **8.** 6.1 _____

9. 5.9 _____   **10.** 4.4 _____

11. 6.7 _____   **12.** 5.5 _____

Round off to the nearest dollar.

13. $1.89 _____   **14.** $5.12 _____

15. $10.25 _____   **16.** $9.09 _____

17. $19.71 _____   **18.** $100.62 _____

19. $56.82 _____   **20.** $10.50 _____

21. $96.20 _____   **22.** $25.75 _____

23. $18.48 _____   **24.** $86.73 _____

Constitution Countdown

Read the passage and fill in the missing dates and words on the time line.

On July 4 in 1776, the United States declared independence from Great Britain, and a new country was born. After the Revolutionary War was over, Americans needed to decide how they would govern themselves. In 1777, they created the Articles of Confederation. Unfortunately, the Articles of Confederation led to a weak government that needed to be changed.

In May of 1787, delegates from all the states met at a convention in Philadelphia, Pennsylvania. They decided to set aside the Articles of Confederation and write a new Constitution. By September of 1787, the new Constitution was accepted by the delegates. But the delegates then had to convince all the states to vote in favor of it! It wasn't until 1788 that New Hampshire voted to accept the Constitution, and the Articles of Confederation were finally replaced. In 1790, Rhode Island became the last state to vote in favor of the Constitution.

TIME LINE				
1776				
The United States declared independence from _____ _____.	The Articles of _____ were created.	In May, delegates met at a convention in _____ _____.	The state of _____ voted to accept the Constitution and the _____ of Confederation were replaced.	_____ _____ became the last state to accept the Constitution.

Marvelous Munchie Mix

Read the recipe for making Marvelous Munchie Mix.
Then answer the questions.

Marvelous Munchie Mix

(Serves 12)

$1\frac{1}{2}$ cups corn flakes

$\frac{1}{2}$ cup raisins

$\frac{1}{3}$ cup dried cranberries

$\frac{3}{4}$ cup peanuts

$\frac{2}{3}$ cup chocolate chips

1 cup mini pretzels

$1\frac{1}{4}$ cups honey

2 tsp. salt

Mix together all ingredients in a large bowl. Store in an airtight container or a plastic bag.

1. You're making Munchie Mix for 48 campers. How many batches of Munchie Mix should you make?

   _____

2. Write how much of each ingredient you will need to serve 48 campers.

   _____ corn flakes

   _____ raisins

   _____ dried cranberries

   _____ peanuts

   _____ chocolate chips

   _____ mini pretzels

   _____ honey

   _____ salt

3. Yikes! 36 more campers showed up! How many batches should you make now?

   _____

4. Write how much of each ingredient you will need to serve all the campers, including the additional 36 who showed up.

   _____ corn flakes

   _____ raisins

   _____ dried cranberries

   _____ peanuts

   _____ chocolate chips

   _____ mini pretzels

   _____ honey

   _____ salt

5. There are 6 cabins at camp. An equal number of campers sleep in each cabin. If each camper gets an individual bag of Munchie Mix, how many bags do you make for each cabin?

   _____

6. If each camper shares a bag of Munchie Mix with one other person, how many bags do you make per cabin?

   _____

Parts of Speech Puzzle

Complete the activity below.

A **hink pink** is a riddle. The answer to the riddle is a pair of words that rhyme. To find the answer to the hink pink, follow these steps:
- Read each sentence.
- Write the word that matches the part of speech in the boxes.
- Then write all the circled letters in the boxes in order at the bottom of the page.

1. Leah plays drums in the school band. (verb)

2. What kind of hobby do you have? (common noun)

3. Mina writes romantic poetry. (adjective)

4. Ben rides go-carts with his brother. (preposition)

5. Jenny volunteers at the art museum. (common noun)

6. You can find Pam happily tending her garden. (adverb)

7. My cousin Ralph enjoys cooking. (proper noun)

8. Dad fixes classic cars inside the garage. (preposition)

9. Juvia paints amazing pictures of animals. (adjective)

10. Everyone should pick a good hobby. (verb)

Hink Pink: What does a crustacean with an injury have?

Answer: A ___ ___ ___ ___ ___ ___   ___ ___ ___ ___

Crystal Caves

Read the passage below. Then complete the activity.

Have you ever seen a crystal vase or glass? You probably noticed that crystal is clear and shiny. It's not at all like a rough, dark rock. And yet, crystals are actually rocks!

Crystals are a type of mineral, and minerals are the building blocks of rocks. An igneous rock is really a big clump of different minerals stuck together. As minerals combine and grow, sometimes they start to change shape. They can develop flat sides with sharp, clear edges. When minerals have lots of space to grow, they form beautiful, large crystals.

Crystals can grow naturally in caves. Some of the largest natural crystals on Earth are in a cave in Mexico. The cave is called the Cave of Swords because the crystals look like giant swords. A nearby cave called Cave of Giant Crystals has crystals that are over 50 feet long!

In the left circle, write some facts or words about crystals. In the right circle, write about rocks. In the middle part, write some facts or details that are true for both rocks and crystals.

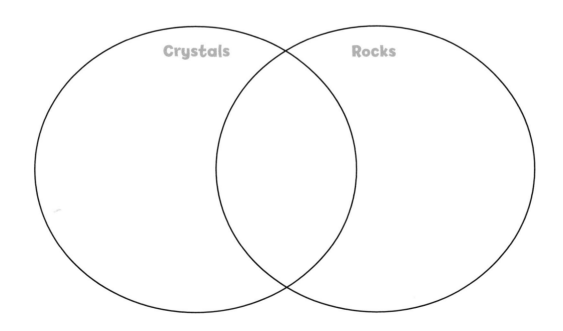

Crystals   Rocks

How to Make a Chocolate Shake

Have an adult help you follow the directions to
make a delicious chocolate shake!

1. Using an ice cream scooper, put 2 scoops of vanilla ice cream in a blender.
2. Measure 1 cup of milk and add it to the blender.
3. Pour 3 tablespoons of chocolate syrup into the blender.
4. Secure the lid on top of the blender and turn on the power.
5. Blend everything together for ten to fifteen seconds.
6. Pour your milkshake into a glass and enjoy!

Fill in the blanks.

Ingredients:

____ scoops vanilla ice cream

____ cups milk

____ tablespoons chocolate syrup

Read each statement and write **true** or **false**.

1. To follow this recipe you need an ice cream scooper, a blender, and a sharp knife.
   _____false_____

2. This recipe calls for chocolate ice cream and milk. _____

3. The recipe tells you to put the ice cream in the blender first, then add the milk.
   _____

4. It is important to turn on the power before securing the lid. _____

5. After blending for ten seconds, you should add the chocolate syrup. _____

6. You should blend everything for ten to fifteen seconds. _____

Team Order

Your tennis coach is ordering lunch for the team.
There are 30 players on the team. This is what they want to order:

$\frac{2}{3}$ want a cheeseburger

$\frac{1}{5}$ want a pizza slice

$\frac{3}{5}$ want a salad

$\frac{1}{3}$ want chicken nuggets

$\frac{1}{2}$ want lemonade

$\frac{1}{6}$ want a corndog

$\frac{2}{5}$ want milk

$\frac{2}{3}$ want an ice cream cone

$\frac{2}{6}$ want apple cake

$\frac{1}{10}$ want bottled water

$\frac{4}{5}$ want french fries

$\frac{2}{5}$ want fruit cups

How much of each food should your coach order?

Quantity	Food

Hunting for Homophones

Homophones are words that sound the same, but they are not spelled the same. Read each word. Then write the word for the picture. These words are homophones.

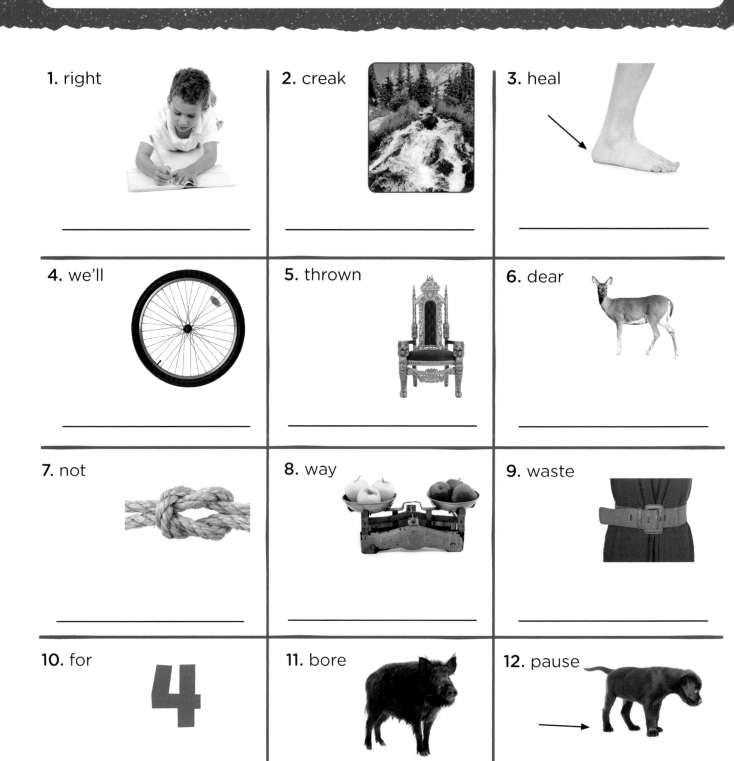

1. right

_____

2. creak

_____

3. heal

_____

4. we'll

_____

5. thrown

_____

6. dear

_____

7. not

_____

8. way

_____

9. waste

_____

10. for

_____

11. bore

_____

12. pause

_____

Martian Multiplication

Multiply to solve each problem. Find the answer below and write the letter.

1. 2320
× 32
P

2. 3105
× 15
T

3. 3251
× 40
E

4. 1243
× 22
L

5. 2164
× 46
T

6. 5340
× 10
A

7. 7252
× 18
L

8. 2407
× 43
I

9. 3245
× 11
S

10. 2431
× 12
N

What does a Martian say when he's organizing a party?

_____ _____ _____ , _____   _____ _____ _____ _____
27,346   130,040 99,544 35,695   74,240 130,536 53,400 29,172

_____ _____ !
103,501   46,575

Number Games

Read the clues, then solve each math problem below.

Clues

1. Each problem has two steps.
2. Use two operation signs (×, −, +, ÷).
3. Use one equals sign (=).

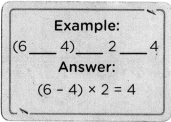

Example:

(6 ____ 4) ____ 2 ____ 4

Answer:

(6 − 4) × 2 = 4

1. 18 ____ (3 ____ 2) ____ 12

2. (60 ____ 6) ____ 3 ____ 30

3. 25 ____ (12 ____ 3) ____ 11

4. 90 ____ (4 ____ 11) ____ 46

5. (20 ____ 5) ____ 9 ____ 36

6. (19 ____ 11) ____ 7 ____ 23

7. (56 ____ 8) ____ 7 ____ 49

8. 42 ____ (6 ____ 5) ____ 12

9. 36 ____ 54 ____ (6 ____ 3)

10. 9 ____ (18 ____ 9) ____ 11

Writing a Paragraph

A **paragraph** must have a **main idea** and **supporting details**.
Read the following paragraph. Circle the main idea, and
write two supporting details below.

The tail of a comet is a beautiful sight to see! People used to think that comets were on fire, but now we know that comets are lumps of ice and dust. When a comet goes streaking past the sun, some of the ice begins to melt. Gas and dust are released to form a long tail that is lit by the sun. This tail streams behind the comet like long, flowing hair. Comets are really millions of miles away, but we can see them from Earth. Usually, a comet's blazing tail helps us see it.

Main Idea:

Comets are made of lumps of ice and dust.

People see comets all the time.

Comets have long, beautiful tails.

Two Supporting Details:

_____

_____

Now write your own paragraph. You can write about your family, a pet, a sport you play, or anything else that interests you. Make sure to include

- a topic sentence
- a main idea
- supporting details

_____

_____

_____

_____

_____

_____

Branches of Government

Complete the activity below.

Executive Branch
This branch makes sure that the laws of the country are obeyed. The president is the head of the Executive branch. The president has helpers called cabinet members.

Judicial Branch
This branch is the court system. It makes sure our laws follow the guidelines in the Constitution. The Supreme Court has nine judges, called Justices. The Chief Justice is the head of the Supreme Court.

Legislative Branch
This branch makes laws for the country. The Senate and the House of Representatives are members of this branch. Together, they make up the US Congress.

Check off which branch of government each person works for.

	Executive	Legislative	Judicial
1. A Supreme Court Justice			✓
2. A senator			
3. A member of the president's cabinet			
4. The Chief Justice			
5. A member of Congress			
6. The president			

Perimeter and Area

Complete the activity below.

Perimeter is the sum of the length of all of a shape's sides. To find perimeter, add all of a shape's sides together. **Area** is the amount of space a shape covers. To find area, multiply a shape's length times the width (l × w). Answers are written in square units (sq. in., sq. ft.). Find the perimeter of each shape. Write the equation. The first one is done for you.

1.

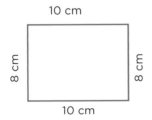

Equation:
10 cm + 10 cm + 8 cm + 8 cm = 36 cm
Perimeter: 36 cm

2.

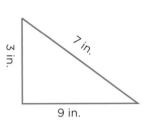

Equation: _____
Perimeter: _____

3.

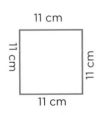

Equation: _____
Perimeter: _____

4.

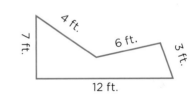

Equation: _____
Perimeter: _____

Find the area of each shape. Write the equation. The first one is done for you.
Hint: You can count the square units to check your answers.

5.

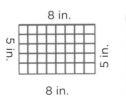

Equation:
8 in. × 5 in. = 40 sq. in.
Area: 40 sq. in.

6.

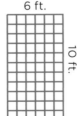

Equation:

_____

Area:

_____

7.

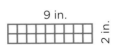

Equation: _____
Area: _____

8.

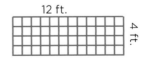

Equation: _____
Area: _____

Mars: The Red Planet

Some words can be confusing. Read the usage for each word.
Then circle the word that best completes each sentence.

There, Their, They're

There is an adverb. It tells where.
Their is a possessive pronoun. It means "belongs to them."
They're is a contraction. It means "they are."

Your, You're

Your is a possessive pronoun. It means "belongs to you."
You're is a contraction. It means "you are."

Its, It's

Its is a possessive pronoun. It means "belongs to it."
It's a contraction. It means "it is."

1. Today (your, you're) going on a trip to Mars!

2. Do you know how Mars got (it's, its) name "the red planet"?

3. (It's, Its) called "the red planet" because it looks red in the sky.

4. Some scientists say (they're, there) sure Mars once had rivers and lakes.

5. (They're, Their) observations make some people think there's life there, too!

6. What is (you're, your) opinion about life on Mars?

7. If life exists (their, there), then maybe Martians are real after all.

8. Maybe (they're, there) little green creatures, like from the movies.

9. Scientists say (it's, its) possible that some form of life may have existed.

10. Do you know that (your, you're) living on the planet most like Mars?

11. Some people think (it's, its) silly to believe in Martians.

12. Only further research will tell whether (they're, their) doubts are correct.

What on Earth Happened?

Read the passage and complete the activity below.

Our Earth is constantly changing! Sometimes these changes happen very quickly, like during an avalanche or flood. But usually these changes happen so slowly that we don't even realize it. It all starts when rocks get worn down from rain, ice, or heat. After the rocks crumble, the particles are carried away by natural forces. This is called erosion. Over time, erosion can flatten mountains or carve out valleys!

Each box shows a different type of erosion. Label the picture with the correct title.

> water erosion   coastal erosion
>
> wind erosion   glacial erosion

1. Ocean waves and currents sweep away sandy shores.

   coastal erosion

2. A giant moving mass of ice can carry rocks and soil away with it.

   _____

3. As rain runs downhill, it carries away soil.

   _____

4. As the wind whips across the desert, it picks up dirt and sand.

   _____

A Magical Myth

Read the story and answer the questions that follow.

Why the Pine Is Green

Most trees have leaves that turn yellow and fall to the ground during the winter, but the needles of a pine tree stay green all winter long. The people of Asia had a story to explain why the pine needles never die.

According to the myth, a long time ago pine needles did turn yellow and die during the winter. During this time, there was a hunter who liked to walk deep in the woods. One day, the hunter wandered into a place he had never seen before. He was very surprised when he saw seven tiny people. The tiny people explained that they washed in magic water that made them immortal. Because of this water, they could never die.

The Immortal People were glad to see the hunter because they needed some help. One of their people was missing! A large animal had carried the person away. The hunter agreed to help find the missing person. He found the animal and returned the tiny person to safety. The Immortal People wanted to thank the hunter. They promised to bring him the magic water so that he could become immortal, too.

The hunter went back to his village and waited. Many days passed. One day, the women in the hunter's village saw the Immortal People walking toward them. They thought the tiny people looked strange because they were so small. The women laughed and laughed at the tiny people.

What do you think happened next? Write your prediction on the lines below.

_____

_____

_____

Here's how the story ends:

The Immortal People did not like to be laughed at. They were very hurt. They decided not to bring the hunter the magic water. Instead, they dumped the water on the ground near some pine trees. So, the pine trees became immortal. This is why pine trees today have green needles that never die. Was your prediction right?

More Magical Myth

See the story on the previous page to answer the questions below.

1. The word *immortal* means:
   a) to be very small
   b) to never die
   c) to never have winter

2. Why did the Immortal People want to thank the hunter?
   a) Because he chased away a large animal.
   b) Because he promised to keep their secret.
   c) Because he helped find the missing person.

3. Why did the village women laugh at the Immortal People?
   a) Because they thought the tiny people were funny.
   b) Because they thought the tiny people looked strange.
   c) Because one of the women told a joke.

4. Why did the Immortal People dump the water on the ground?
   a) Because they were angry with the hunter.
   b) Because they were hurt that the women laughed at them.
   c) Because they wanted the pine trees to stay green.

5. The purpose of the myth is
   a) To explain why pine needles stay green all winter long.
   b) To show people why pine trees are important.
   c) To teach people how to water pine trees.

6. Number the sentences 1 through 6 to show the order of events.
   ____ The village women laughed at the Immortal People.
   ____ The hunter discovered a group of tiny people deep in the woods.
   ____ The Immortal People promised they would bring the hunter some magic water.
   ____ The hunter helped return the missing person to the group of Immortal People.
   ____ The Immortal People dumped the magic water on the ground.
   ____ The hunter waited and waited for the Immortal People to bring the water.

Here Comes the Ice Cream Truck

How many times did the ice cream truck stop on each street?
Use the data below to fill in the chart. Each truck stands for 2 stops.
Then answer the questions below.

Elm Street   🚚 🚚

Pinewood Avenue   🚚 🚚

Main Street   🚚 🚚 🚚 🚚 🚚

Windy Lane   🚚

Cherry Avenue   🚚 🚚 🚚

10					
8					
6					
4					
2					
0	Elm St.	Main St.	Cherry Ave.	Pinewood Ave.	Windy Ln.

1. On which street did the ice cream truck make the most stops?

_____

2. On which street did the ice cream truck make the fewest stops?

_____

3. On which two streets did the ice cream truck make the same number of stops?

_____ and _____

4. How many more stops did the truck make on Main St. than Cherry Ave.?

_____

5. How many stops total did the truck make on Elm St. and Windy Ln.?

_____

6. How many stops did the truck make altogether on all the streets?

_____

Writing Well

Good writing contains specific details and descriptions.
To make simple sentences even better, ask yourself these questions:
Who? What? Where? When? Why? How?

Example:

I love pizza.

What kind?   **Where?**   **When?**

pepperoni and olive   from Enzo's   after a long day at school

New Sentence:

I love pepperoni and olive pizza from Enzo's after a long day at school.

Now, try your hand at making these sentences better.
Answer the questions shown, then write your new sentence.

1. The children sang.

What kind? _____ How? _____ Where? _____

_____

2. The plane soared.

How? _____ Where? _____ When? _____

_____

3. The dog barked.

What kind? _____ How? _____ Where? _____

_____

4. The wind blew.

How? _____ **What?** _____ When? _____

_____

5. The baby cried.

Why? _____ Where? _____ When? _____

_____

6. The bunny jumped.

What kind? _____ How? _____ Why? _____

_____

Book Survey

You are taking a survey to find out which kinds of books your friends like best. Fill in the graph using the clues below. (Color a bar up to the correct number to show your results.) Then answer the questions.

- 15 friends like nonfiction best.
- 9 friends like fantasy best.
- $\frac{1}{3}$ as many friends like mystery as like fantasy best.
- If you add the number of friends who like fantasy and poetry together, you'll find out how many like adventure best.
- Twice as many friends like science fiction as like mystery best.
- 4 people like poetry best.

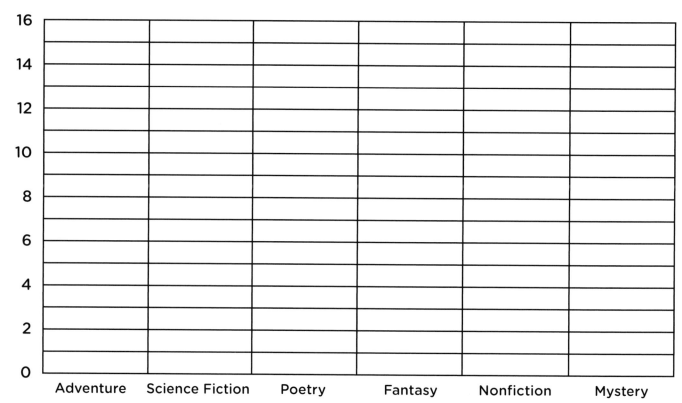

1. Which kind of book is the most favorite? _____
   Least favorite? _____
2. How many friends like poetry and science fiction books together? _____
3. How many fewer friends like fantasy than nonfiction? _____
4. How many more friends like adventure than mystery? _____
5. How many friends did you survey altogether? _____

Describe It in Detail

Think of a special place you like to visit. It could be a vacation spot, like the mountains. It could be your grandparents' house. Choose a place that has special meaning to you. Then use your five senses to describe it in detail. Fill in the chart below.

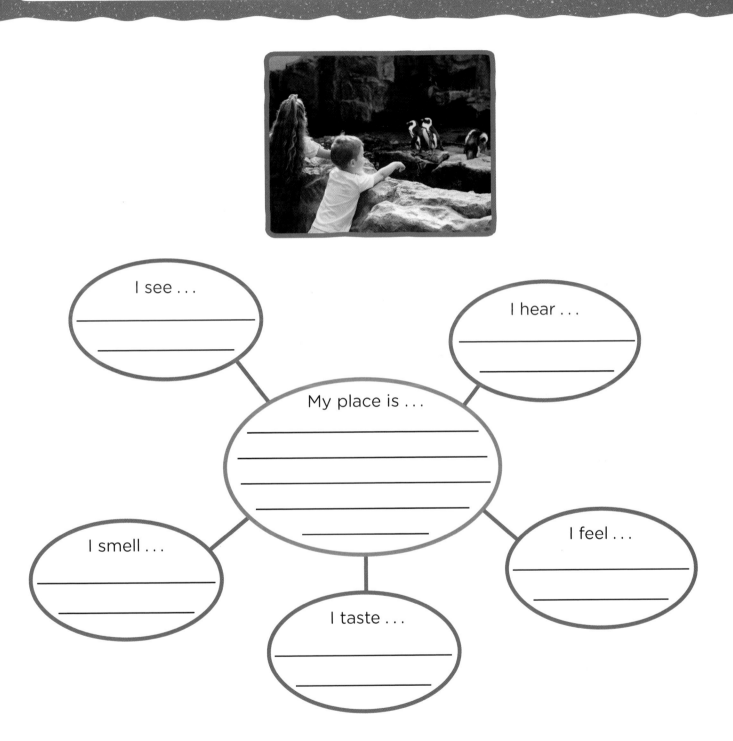

I see . . .

I hear . . .

My place is . . .

I smell . . .

I feel . . .

I taste . . .

On another sheet of paper, use your details to write a descriptive paragraph. Your description should paint a picture for the reader. Remember to use your five senses!

Graph Giggles

An **ordered pair** of numbers is used to locate a point. The first number shows how many units across. The second number shows how many units up. Find each ordered pair on the grid and write the letter on the line.

Example: 2,1

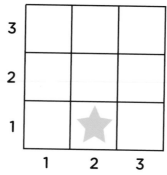

6	V	D	U	A	L	B
5	N	O	N	S	R	U
4	J	M	C	I	H	N
3	X	T	W	L	I	O
2	A	E	O	F	M	P
1	Z	D	P	G	Y	E
	1	2	3	4	5	6

Why was the grid so shy?

Because people were always __ __ __ __ __ __ __ __

at him!   (6,2) (3,2) (5,3) (1,5) (2,3) (4,4) (3,5) (4,1)

Two Kinds of Government

Read about federal and state governments.
Then list which powers each government has in the diagram below.

You may sometimes see two flags flying on a flagpole. These are the American flag and your state flag. That's because both the country and the states have their own governments. Each one has certain powers.

The government for the whole country is called the federal government. Only the federal government has the power to print money. The federal government also handles our country's relationships with other countries. This is called foreign policy. Sometimes, the federal government makes deals, or treaties, with other nations. It also has to protect the country, so it oversees the army and navy. The US Postal Service is run by the federal government, too.

The state government has the power to hold elections for local governments. It gives out licenses for lots of different things—business, driving, marriage, and even fishing! It also votes on whether changes should be made to the Constitution.

Shared powers are things that both federal and state governments do. They both have to collect taxes, build roads, set up courts, and make and enforce laws to protect the health and safety of the people!

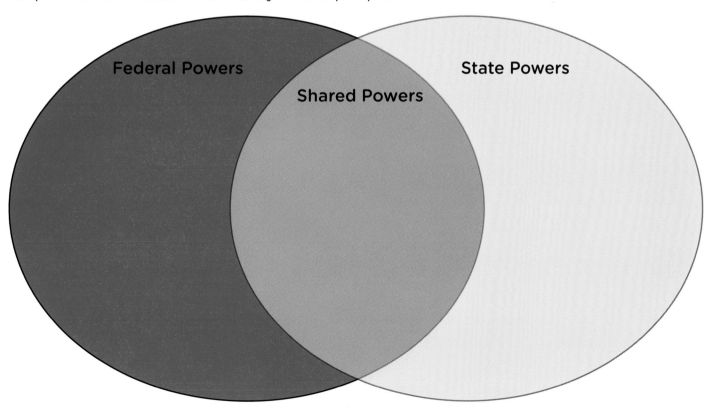

Federal Powers

Shared Powers

State Powers

Summer Jobs

Jenny, Ava, Hunter, Corey, and Daniel are all working summer jobs. The jobs are mowing lawns, pet sitting, tutoring, washing cars, and delivering newspapers. Read the clues and check off each child's summer job.

- Ava uses leashes and toys when she works.
- Hunter performs his job outside.
- Jenna uses soap and towels for her job.
- Daniel needs a bike for his job.

	Mowing Lawns	Pet Sitting	Tutoring	Washing Cars	Delivering Newspapers
Jenna					
Ava					
Hunter					
Corey					
Daniel					

Dictionary Entries

A **dictionary** can help you find the meanings and the spellings of words.
Words are listed in alphabetical order.

Entries look like this:

cab (kab) *noun* 1. A car that takes people from place to place.
Milo took a cab across town. 2. The driver's area of a large truck or machine.

Some elements help the reader better understand each word:

ENTRY WORD   HOW TO SAY
SYLLABLES   THE WORD
                        PART OF SPEECH

cab (kab) *noun* 1. A car that takes people from place to place.
Milo took a cab across town. 2. The driver's area of a large truck or machine.

SAMPLE SENTENCE   DEFINITION (THERE CAN BE MORE THAN ONE.)

Answer the following questions about each entry word.

per•form (pur-form) *verb* 1. To do something or carry out something. 2. To give a show in public.

1. What part of speech is **perform**? _____

2. How many syllables are in the word **perform**? _____

3. Write a sample sentence using the second meaning of **perform**.

_____

sweet (swēt) *adjective* 1. Tastes of sugar or honey. 2. Gentle and kind. *My friend Lan is a sweet person.*
noun 3. Piece of candy or other sweet-tasting food.

4. What part of speech is the second definition? _____

5. How many definitions does the word **sweet** have? _____

6. Write a sample sentence using the first meaning of **sweet**.

_____

bril•liant (bril-yuhnt) *adjective* 1. Shines very brightly. 2. Very smart. 3. Terrific, wonderful. *The singer gave a brilliant performance.*

7. How many syllables are in the word **brilliant**? _____

8. Which definition is the sample sentence? _____

9. Write a sample sentence using the second meaning of **brilliant**.

_____

Book Report!

It's time to write your very own book report! First, choose a book that tells a story. After you read it, fill in the information below.

Book title: _____

Author: _____

The book is about _____

The characters are _____
_____

The setting of the story is _____

Here's what happened in the story. First, _____
_____

Next, _____

Finally, _____

My favorite part was when _____
_____
_____

I liked this book because _____
_____
_____

Playing the Odds

Probability is a way to guess, or estimate, an answer to a problem.
It can help you come close to an answer without actually solving a problem.

Use the spinner to answer the questions. Circle your answer.

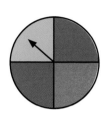

1. How many times will the spinner land on purple?

a) 20%   b) 10%   c) 70%   d) 50%

2. How many times will the spinner land on red or green?

a) $\frac{1}{3}$ b) $\frac{1}{2}$ c) $\frac{1}{4}$ d) $\frac{3}{4}$

3. Red has the same chance as:

a) purple   b) green

c) both green   d) all of the above
   and purple

4. How many times will the spinner land on green?

a) $\frac{1}{2}$ b) $\frac{2}{4}$

c) $\frac{1}{4}$ d) none of the above

There are six numbers on a die: 1, 2, 3, 4, 5, 6.

5. You have 4 dice. You roll three 5s on your first roll. What is the probability that you will roll a 3 with your remaining die?

a) $\frac{1}{6}$ b) $\frac{3}{6}$

c) $\frac{2}{4}$ d) $\frac{1}{4}$

6. You have 1 die. What is the probability that you will roll a 2, 4, or 6 on the first roll?

a) $\frac{6}{6}$ b) $\frac{1}{6}$

c) $\frac{3}{6}$ d) $\frac{4}{6}$

Sammy the seal juggles 8 balls on his nose.

7. What is the probability that he will drop a yellow ball?

a) $\frac{3}{8}$ b) $\frac{2}{4}$

c) $\frac{4}{8}$ d) $\frac{1}{8}$

8. What is the probability that he will drop a blue ball?

a) $\frac{3}{8}$ b) $\frac{5}{8}$

c) $\frac{8}{8}$ d) $\frac{1}{2}$

A Biography Of...

Complete the activity below.

A **biography** tells the story of another person's life. Choose a person whose life story you think would be interesting to tell. This could be a friend, a neighbor, a grandparent, a teacher, a coach, or another community member. Conduct an interview by asking this person the following questions. Then write your biography on another piece of paper based on the person's answers.

This is a biography of: _____

Where do you live? _____

How old are you? _____

Where did you grow up? _____

What was your favorite thing about school?

_____

_____

What special activities did you do? _____

_____

Name three important events in your life, and tell why each was important.

1. _____

_____

2. _____

_____

3. _____

_____

If you could change one thing in your life, what would it be? _____

_____

If you had one wish, what would it be?

_____

_____

President's Page

Choose an American president whom you would like to learn more about.
Then go to the library and read about that president in an encyclopedia.
Fill in the information below. And you'll have a report!

President's name: _____

During what years did this president serve? _____

Birthplace: _____

Birthdate: _____

When _____ _____ was young, he
　　　　first name　　　　last name

_____

As he got older, he _____

_____

He became president in _____

Here are some of the important things he did when he was president:

_____
_____
_____

If I could meet this president, this is what I would ask him:

_____
_____
_____

Home Sweet Home

Look at the layouts of this house. Read the measurements. Then answer the questions.

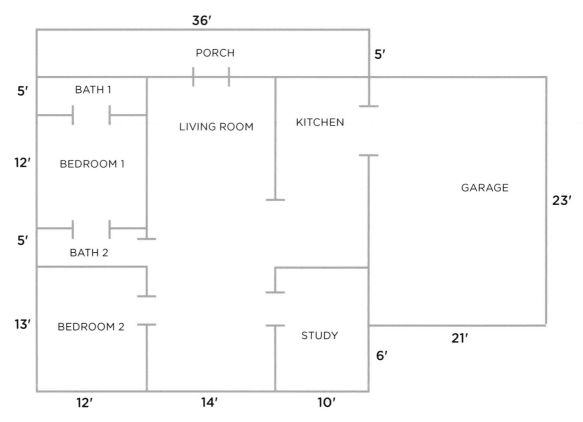

1. What are the perimeter and the area of the living room?
   Perimeter = _____
   Area = _____

2. What are the perimeter and the area of the garage?
   Perimeter = _____
   Area = _____

3. What are the perimeter and the area of bedroom 1?
   Perimeter = _____
   Area = _____

4. What is the perimeter of bedroom 1 and bathroom 1 put together?
   Perimeter = _____

5. What is the perimeter of bedroom 2 and the study put together?
   Perimeter = _____

6. What are the perimeter and the area of the porch?
   Perimeter = _____
   Area = _____

7. What is the perimeter of the entire house and porch, without the garage?
   Perimeter = _____

8. What is the area of the entire house, without the garage or porch?
   Area = _____

Olympics: Then and Now

Read the passage below. Then answer the questions.

The Olympic games have been around a long time. They first began in Greece in 776 BCE. That is more than 2,700 years ago! They took place every fourth summer in the city of Olympia. Only free men who spoke Greek could compete. Women could not compete at all. Maybe this is because the men competed without clothes! Back then there were only a few events. Some of them were the same as today. These included foot races, wrestling, boxing, and jumping. Others were different, though, like chariot races. Winners did not receive medals, but they were given wreaths of olive leaves.

The Olympic games have changed a lot over the years. Today there are both summer and winter games. Now both men and women can compete. Women usually make up half of the teams. More than 200 different countries compete, not just one. Each Olympics is held in a different city around the world. There are many more sports today. In the winter and the summer Olympics there are more than 35 different sports.

1. In what year and what city did the first Olympics take place? _____

2. Compare women's roles in ancient games to modern games.

_____

_____

3. What did ancient winners get for a prize? _____

4. What do today's winners get for a prize? _____

5. Name three sports played in both the ancient and the modern games.

_____

6. Write three ways the modern games are different from the ancient games.

_____

_____

_____

Rounding, Rounding, All Around

Rounding numbers is easy! Here's how you do it.

Example: Round 10,554 to the nearest hundred.
- Look at the number to the right of the hundreds place. It is a 5.
- If the number is 5 or greater, round up.
- If the number is 4 or less, round down.

Answer: 10,600

Round these numbers.

1. 1,633 to the nearest ten

_____

2. 7,790 to the nearest hundred

_____

3. 9,488 to the nearest thousand

_____

4. 12,165 to the nearest hundred

_____

5. 37,535 to the nearest thousand

_____

6. 66,329 to the nearest hundred

_____

7. 96,466 to the nearest ten

_____

8. 54,937 to the nearest thousand

_____

9. 463,489 to the nearest thousand

_____

10. 199,061 to the nearest ten thousand

_____

Now, go back to your answers. Circle every number in the thousands place. Use the secret code to find out the answer to the following question. Write the letter that goes with each number, in order, on the lines below.

0 = N   1 = T   2 = B   3 = O   4 = E

5 = I   6 = L   7 = W   8 = I   9 = O

 How many pennies does it take to go around Earth?

___ ___ ___   ___ ___ ___ ___ ___ ___

Answer Key

Page 4
Person:
Josh Baker
Carlos Gomez
friend
boys
forest ranger
campers
Place:
Coal Canyon
meadow
camp
Thing:
bear
hike
summer
lunch
brush
food
feet
bears

Page 5
1. b
2. c
3. false
4. true
5. false
6. true

Page 6
1. 2 x 3 = 6
2. 2 x 4 = 8
3. 2 x 10 = 20
4. 2 x 8 = 16
5. 2 x 12 = 24
6. 2 x 6 = 12
7. 2 x 7 = 14
8. 2 x 1 = 2
9. 2 x 11 = 22
10. 2 x 2 = 4
11. 2 x 5 = 10
12. 2 x 9 = 18

Page 7
1. sour
2. awake
3. careful
4. over
5. spend
6. winter
7. calm
8. horrible
9. noisy
10. slowly

Page 8
2. 60
3. 420
4. 6,550
5. 850
7. 700
8. 8,200
9. 1,400
10. 100
12. 4,000
13. 3,000
14. 7,000
15. 1,000

Page 9

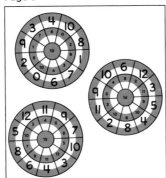

Page 10
1. tail
2. scent
3. aunt
4. piece
5. made
6. rode
7. clothes
8. blue
9. break
10. their

Page 11
Dear Grandma,
I just got the card you sent me for my birthday. Yesterday I turned eight years old. We went on a hike through the woods. It was a beautiful day, and the scent of wildflowers was in the air. We even saw a deer! We came to a creek with clear, blue water. As we walked across the bridge, I heard it creak. At lunchtime, we stopped for a picnic and ate sandwiches and chips. We threw away all our trash. When we got home, I blew out the candles on my birthday cake. I wished that I could go another hike for my birthday next year!
1. clothes
2. red
3. bear
4. new
5. pair

Page 12
Across:
2. 30
4. 12
6. 18
7. 3
8. 15
10. 6
11. 33

Down:
1. 27
3. 21
4. 24
5. 36
9. 9

Page 13
Answers will vary.

Page 14
2. 1
3. 2
4. 4
5. b
6. b
7. Answers will vary.

Page 15

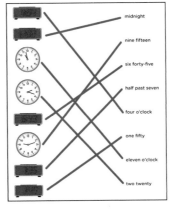

Page 16
1. Sept.
2. Nov.
3. Sun.
4. Jan.
5. Mr.
6. Fri.
7. Dr.
8. Sr.
9. Thurs.
10. Dec.
11. Aug.
12. Wed.
13. Jr.
14. Feb.
15. Oct.
16. Sat.
17. Tues.
18. Apr.
19. Mrs.
20. Mon.

Page 17

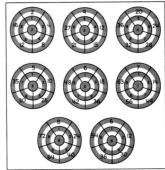

Page 18
Row 1: 48, 36, 4, 28, 44, 16
Row 2: 40, 32, 8, 24, 12, 20
Cross out the following numbers:
Bunch 1: 44, 16, 32, 8, 24
Bunch 2: 12, 36, 48, 4, 28, 40, 20
Bunch 1 has the most balloons left.

Page 19
1. He was 18 years old.
2. He enjoyed hiking in the forest and swimming in the rivers.
3. 1797
4. He put fences around them.
5. The trees had turned into huge apple orchards.

Page 20
2. Light travels in a straight line.
3. Sunlight contains all the colors of the rainbow.
4. Sunlight can be blocked to create shadows.

Page 21
2. un
3. re
4. un
5. dis
6. un
7. re
8. dis
9. dis
10. e
11. f
12. g
13. i
14. c
15. d
16. b
17. h
18. a

Page 22
1. 4 quarters, 3 dimes, 1 nickel, 0 pennies
2. 4 quarters, 2 dimes, 2 nickels, 2 pennies
3. 8 quarters, 0 dimes, 2 nickels, 0 pennies
4. 3 quarters, 5 dimes, 0 nickels, 0 pennies
5. 6 quarters, 1 dime, 2 nickels, 3 pennies
6. 0 quarters, 1 dime, 6 nickels, 1 penny
7. 2 quarters, 2 dimes, 3 nickels, 0 pennies
8. 1 quarter, 2 dimes, 3 nickels, 2 pennies

Page 23
2. 5 x 2 = 10, 2 x 5 = 10
   5 x 2 = 2 x 5
3. 7 x 5 = 35, 5 x 7 = 35
   7 x 5 = 5 x 7
4. 6 x 4 = 24, 4 x 6 = 24
   6 x 4 = 4 x 6
5. 7 x 8 = 56, 8 x 7 = 56
   7 x 8 = 8 x 7
6. 9 x 3 = 27, 3 x 9 = 27
   9 x 3 = 3 x 9

Page 24
1. ten
2. sixty
3. thirty
4. fifteen
5. fifty
6. forty
7. fifty-five
8. thirty-five
9. twenty
10. five
11. forty-five
12. twenty-five
THE LETTER E

Page 25
1. silent, wallet
2. crane, meeting
3. join, bleed
4. sneeze, pilot
5. ache, hit
6. eel, ride
7. vein, down
8. goat, offer

Page 26
2. ÷
3. ÷
4. ÷
5. ×
6. ÷
7. ×
8. ÷

Page 27
2. then
3. now
4. now
5. now
6. then

Page 28
1.

2.

3. 6
4. 1
5. 3
6. 5

Page 29
1. Rains swept the herd down the river.
2. Wildlife rangers found him.
3. They took him to Haller Park Animal Center.
4. Mzee is a giant male tortoise.
5. Because Mzee is big and gray like a hippo.

Page 30
2. koala
3. turtle
4. porcupine
5. skunk
6. elephant

Page 31
1. big, bitter
2. bill; Sentences will vary.
3. bill, bite
4. biscuit, bitter
5. bid, blame
6. bin, biscuit
7. Sentences will vary.
8. birth, blade, black, bike

Page 32
Row 1: 60, 12, 36, 24, 66, 54
Row 2: 18, 48, 72, 42, 6, 30
Acorns circled: 72, 30, 66, 12, 60, 36, 18, 24, 42, 54, 6, 48
You gathered 12 acorns.

Page 33
1. Whales are not fish; they are mammals. T
2. Pet the dolphins gently. C
3. What kind of food do crabs eat? A
4. Don't touch anything in the tide pools. C
5. Wow, that starfish grew a new leg! E
6. Sharks do not have any bones in their bodies. T
7. Do whales lay eggs or have live babies? A
8. Ouch, that shark tooth is sharp! E
Sentences will vary.

Page 34
1. 1
2. Answers will vary.
3. 4, 8
4. 10
5. c

Page 35
2. $\frac{4}{6}$
3. $\frac{2}{10}$
4. $\frac{3}{6}$
5. $\frac{2}{8}$
6. $\frac{3}{9}$
7. $\frac{4}{10}$
8. $\frac{2}{12}$
10. P
11. I
12. P
13. P

Page 36
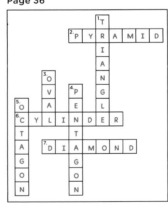

Page 37
1. "I got a job at the animal shelter," Jenny said.
2. The Caring Friends Animal Shelter is in Shasta Park.
3. "How many people work at the shelter?" Dad asked.
4. Caring Friends hires new workers in January and June.
5. The shelter takes in cats, dogs, rabbits, snakes, and birds.
6. Mia has worked at Caring Friends since May 11, 2002.
7. Dr. Brown works there on Mondays, Fridays, and Saturdays.
8. Carlos has been missing his dog Max since the Fourth of July.
9. Carlos asked, "Do you think Max might be at the shelter?"
10. The Gomez family finally found Max on Labor Day.

Page 38
2. $\frac{7}{10}$; .7
3. $\frac{2}{10}$; .2
4. $\frac{1}{4} = \frac{25}{100}$; .25
5. $\frac{2}{4} = \frac{50}{100}$; .50
6. $\frac{3}{4} = \frac{75}{100}$; .75

Page 39
1. b
2. a
3. c
4. c, a, d, b

Page 40
Row 1: 42, 7, 84, 70, 56, 28
Row 2: 63, 35, 21, 77, 14, 49

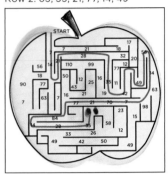

Page 41
2. true
3. false
4. true
5. false
6. true

Page 42
2. c
3. g
4. h
5. a
6. d
7. e
8. b
9. gentle, rough
10. loud, quiet
11. asleep, awake
12. far, near

Page 43
1. <
2. >
3. >
4. =
5. >
6. >
7. <
8. <
9. =
10. =
11. =
12. >
13. >
14. <
15. =
16. <